Inside Out

Theodore Clymer

Donald J. Bissett
Gretchen Wulfing

Consultants

William E. Blanton EVALUATION

Milton D. Jacobson READABILITY

Ken Johnson LANGUAGE

Roger W. Shuy LINGUISTICS

E. Paul Torrance CREATIVITY

GINN AND COMPANY
A Xerox Education Company

Acknowledgments

Grateful acknowledgment is made to the following publishers, authors, and agents for permission to use and adapt copyrighted materials:

Abelard-Schuman Limited for "Little Wolf." Copyright © 1965 by Ann McGovern. Reprinted from *Little Wolf* by Ann McGovern by permission of Abelard-Schuman Limited, an Intext publisher.

Addison-Wesley Publishing Company, Inc., for "The Fastest Quitter in Town." Adapted from *The Fastest Quitter in Town,* text © 1972, by Phyllis Green, a Young Scott Book, by permission of Addison-Wesley Publishing Company.

Thomas Y. Crowell Company, Inc., for "The Dancing Stars." From *The Dancing Stars* by Anne Rockwell. Copyright © 1972 by Anne Rockwell, with permission of Thomas Y. Crowell Company, Inc., publisher.

Delacorte Press for *The Strange Story of the Frog Who Became a Prince,* by Elinor Horwitz, copyright © 1971 by Elinor Horwitz. Reprinted with permission of Delacorte Press.

Follett Publishing Company for *Dragon Stew,* copyright © 1969, by Tom McGowen. Used by permission of Follett Publishing Company, a division of Follett Corporation.

Harper & Row, Publishers, Inc., for the poem "Robert, Who Is Often A Stranger to Himself" from *Bronzeville Boys and Girls* by Gwendolyn Brooks. Copyright ©, 1956 by Gwendolyn Brooks Blakely. Reprinted by permission of Harper & Row, Publishers, Inc.

Holt, Rinehart and Winston, Inc., for "A Pocketful of Cricket" from *A Pocketful of Cricket* by Rebecca Caudill. Text copyright © 1964 by Rebecca Caudill. Abridged by permission of Holt, Rinehart and Winston, Inc.

Little, Brown and Company for the adaptation of "George." Copyright, ©, 1956, by Phyllis Rowand. From *George* by Phyllis Rowand, by permission of Little, Brown and Co.

Macmillan Publishing Co., Inc., for *Amigo,* text copyright © 1963 Byrd Baylor Schweitzer, illustrations copyright © 1963 Garth Williams. Reprinted by arrangement with Macmillan Publishing Co., Inc.

McGraw-Hill Book Company for "Discovering Dinosaurs," "Whatever Happened to All Those Dinosaurs?" and "Solving the Puzzle." All adapted from *Discovering Dinosaurs* by Glenn O. Blough. Copyright © 1960 by Glenn O. Blough. Used with permission of McGraw-Hill Book Company. Also for the poem "When Dinosaurs Were Roaming." Abridged from *A Dozen Dinosaurs* by Richard Armour. Copyright © 1967 by Richard Armour and Paul Galdone. Used with permission of McGraw-Hill Book Company.

G. P. Putnam's Sons for "Dinosaur Differences." Adaptation by permission of G. P. Putnam's Sons from *In the Time of the Dinosaurs* by William Wise. Copyright © 1963 by William Wise. Also for "Dooly and the Snortsnoot." Adaptation by permission of G. P. Putnam's Sons from *Dooly and the Snortsnoot* by Jack Kent. Copyright © 1972 by Jack Kent.

Random House, Inc., for "The Cool Ride in the Sky" adapted by permission of Alfred A. Knopf, Inc. from *The Cool Ride in the Sky,* by Diane Wolkstein. Copyright © 1973 by Diane Wolkstein. Also for "How Do We Know about Dinosaurs?" Adapted by permission of Random House, Inc. from *In the Days of the Dinosaurs,* by Roy Chapman Andrews. Copyright © 1959 by Roy Chapman Andrews. Also for "Lonely Maria." Adapted by permission of Pantheon Books, a Division of Random House, Inc., from *Lonely Maria,* by Elizabeth Coatsworth. Copyright © 1960 by Pantheon Books, Inc. Also for the poem "Lemons and Apples" from *Woody and Me,* by Mary Neville. Copyright © 1966 by Mary Neville Woodrich and Ronni Solbert. Reprinted by permission of Pantheon Books, a Division of Random House, Inc. and Mary Neville Woodrich.

Simon & Schuster, Inc., for the poem "Worm" from *A Little Book of Little Beasts* by Mary Ann Hoberman. Copyright © 1973, by Mary Ann Hoberman. Reprinted by permission of Simon and Schuster, Children's Book Division.

Henry Z. Walck, Inc., for the poem "The Talking Tiger" by Arnold Spilka from *A Lion I Can Do Without.* Copyright © 1964 by Arnold Spilka. Used by permission of Henry Z. Walck, Inc.

Curtis Brown, Ltd., New York, for "The Cool Ride in the Sky" from *The Cool Ride in the Sky* by Diane Wolkstein. Reprinted by permission of Curtis Brown, Ltd., and World's

Work Ltd. Copyright © 1973 by Diane Wolkstein. Also for "The Dancing Stars" from *The Dancing Stars* by Anne Rockwell. Reprinted by permission of Curtis Brown, Ltd. Copyright © 1972 by Anne Rockwell.

Garrard Publishing Company for "Slue-Foot Sue the Rainmaker" which is an adaptation from the book, *Pecos Bill and the Long Lasso*, by Elizabeth and Carl Carmer. Published by arrangement with Garrard Publishing Co., Champaign, Illinois.

Macrae Smith Company for the play "Giant of the Timber" by Nellie McCaslin, adapted from her book *Tall Tales and Tall Men*. Used by permission of the publisher.

Mary Britton Miller for the poem "Cat" from her book *Menagerie*. Used by permission of the author.

Russell & Volkening, Inc., for the poem "Fish" from *Hello and Goodbye* by Mary Ann Hoberman. Reprinted by permission of Russell & Volkening, Inc. Copyright © 1959 by Mary Ann Hoberman.

The Seabury Press for *The Thief Who Hugged a Moonbeam* by Harold Berson. Copyright © 1972 by Harold Berson. Reprinted by permission of The Seabury Press, New York, publisher of the original picture book version.

Albert Whitman & Company for "End of the Line" adapted from *End of the Line* by Janice May Udry, copyright 1962 by Albert Whitman & Company. Reprinted by permission. Also for "What Mary Jo Wanted" adapted from *What Mary Jo Wanted* by Janice May Udry, copyright 1968 by Janice May Udry. Reprinted by permission of the Albert Whitman Company.

Windmill Productions, Inc., for excerpts on page 119 from *C D B!* by William Steig. Copyright © 1968 by William Steig. Used by permission of the publisher.

World's Work Ltd., England, for *Amigo* by Byrd Baylor Schweitzer. Publishers in the British Commonwealth. All Rights Reserved. Also for the poem "When Dinosaurs Were Roaming," abridged from *A Dozen Dinosaurs* by Richard Armour. Used by permission.

Illustrations and photographs were provided by the following: American Museum of Natural History (216); Mark Bellerose (46–60); Jane Caminos (84–99); Guy Dannella (284–300); Blair Drawson (100–116); Forbes Library, Northhampton (225); Johnathan Goell (45); Judy Sue Goodwin (82–83); Diane de Groat (158–180); Tim and Greg Hildebrandt (76–81); Bruce Hunter—American Museum of Natural History (226); Mark Kelley (117, 258–259); True Kelley (282, 283); Kies de Kiefte (270–281); Ted Lewin (19); Richard Loehle (20–31); Ray Mason (198–215); Lady McCrady (156, 157); Jon McIntosh (64–75); Eleanor Mill (120–133); Leslie Morrill (135–155); Sol Murdocca (134); Dr. David Nathan (219); Bill Ogden (260–269); Ted Rand (32–43); C. R. Schaff—Museum of Comparative Zoology, Harvard University (230); Joel Snyder (194–197, 217, 218, 220–224, 231–237); Stock Boston (227); Karl W. Struecklen (8–18); Ed Taber (248–257); George Ulrich (342–352); Dr. C. Vaurie—American Museum of Natural History (229); Christine Westerberg (239–244).

The cover and unit introduction pages were designed by Gregory Fossella Associates.

Contents

6

Mirror, Mirror

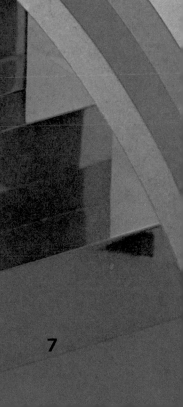

Little Wolf

It is morning.
The sun begins to rise.

The sun rises higher
and higher in the sky.
It shines on all the houses
of the Indian tribe.

The sun wakes up the mother—Flower Wolf.
And the father—Hunt Wolf.
And the old grandfather—Wise Wolf.
And the boy—Little Wolf.

Another day has come.
Flower Wolf will cook.
Hunt Wolf will hunt.
Wise Wolf will sit by the fire.

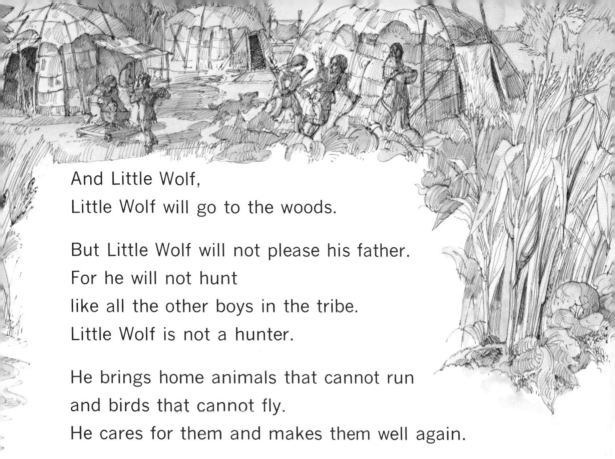

And Little Wolf,
Little Wolf will go to the woods.

But Little Wolf will not please his father.
For he will not hunt
like all the other boys in the tribe.
Little Wolf is not a hunter.

He brings home animals that cannot run
and birds that cannot fly.
He cares for them and makes them well again.

Now Hunt Wolf roars
like the angry thunder god.
"Today, you will hunt!"
he commands Little Wolf.
Little Wolf looks up at his father.

"You are brave," his father says.
"I have seen you wrestle with Big Knife.
But what good is your bravery if you do not
face the sharp antlers of the deer?

"You are swift.
I have seen you race Fast-as-the-Wind.
But what good is your swiftness
if you do not follow the fleeing rabbit?

"You are wise.
You know when rain will fall
and where the big fish swim.
But what good is your wisdom
if you do not trick the sly fox?

"You are brave. And swift. And wise.
You are all these things.
But all these things are nothing
if you do not hunt!"

Now Wise Wolf speaks.
"I know we must kill animals," he says.
"Our people would die if we did not hunt for food.
But let the boy be.
There are other ways."

Hunt Wolf shakes his head.
"No! My son shames me."

"Go now!" he tells Little Wolf.
"And come home when you have killed a deer
or a rabbit or a fox."

So Little Wolf takes his bow and arrow
and leaves his house.
He walks by the houses of all the hunters.
He walks by the Chief's house.
He sees the Chief's only son, Brave Bear.
Brave Bear is very small,
but he is going to be a mighty hunter.

Little Wolf greets the Chief and his son.
But they do not speak to him,
for Little Wolf is not a hunter
like all the other boys in the tribe.

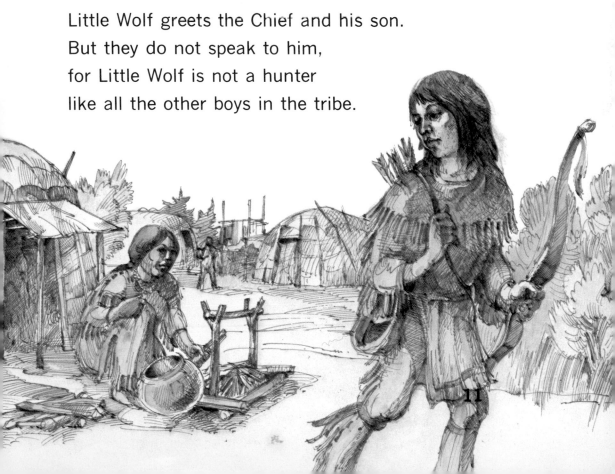

11

Little Wolf goes to the woods.
Everything is very green.
Everything is very quiet.

He knows the woods well.
Wise Wolf has taught him the ways of the woods.
He has taught him about the animals
and about the plants that grow
in the green, quiet woods.
Plants that make men sick,
and plants that make men well.

Soon Little Wolf sees two big brown eyes.
The big brown eyes of a deer.
Little Wolf throws down his bow and arrow.
"How can I be a hunter?" he asks softly.
"How can I be a hunter, if I have to kill you?"

The deer is dark brown velvet running deep
into the woods.

Then Little Wolf sees a round white tail.
The round white tail of a rabbit.
"I will not be a hunter," he says softly.
"I will not be a hunter if I have to kill you."

The rabbit is a quick quiver in the grass,
and is gone.

Then Little Wolf sees a long nose.
The long nose of a fox.
"Never, never will I hunt," he says.
"Never, never will I hunt if I have to kill you."
Then Little Wolf sees the tail of the fox.
It is caught in a trap.
Little Wolf opens the trap and sets the fox free.

The fox is a bounding blur of bright copper.

Now it is night. The moon begins to rise.
The moon rises higher and higher in the sky.
It shines on all the houses of the Indian tribe.

The moon shines on the mother—Flower Wolf.
And on the father—Hunt Wolf.
And on the old grandfather—Wise Wolf.

And on the boy—Little Wolf.

Little Wolf is leaving the woods.
The dark quiet woods.
The trees standing close to the moon.
The plants sleeping near to the earth.

Little Wolf has nothing to show his father.
No deer. No rabbit. No fox.
But he is going home.

Then, in the dark quiet night, he hears a cry.
Little Wolf moves quickly, quietly.
He follows the sound of the cry.

There, under the giant oak,
lies Brave Bear, the Chief's only son.

Brave Bear cries out, "I am dying.
The pain is like a hundred arrows
shooting through me."

Little Wolf sees some berries lying near.
He knows these are berries that make men sick.
He knows Brave Bear has eaten the berries.

"Run for help," Brave Bear moans.
"Run for my father—hurry!"

15

"I can help you," Little Wolf says.
"You?" Brave Bear says.
"What can *you* do? My father says
you cannot even hunt!"

Little Wolf says, "I know the secrets
of the woods.
I can help you."

Little Wolf leaves Brave Bear.
Soon, he returns with grasses and herbs.

"Eat these," Little Wolf says,
"and you will be well
when the sun shines again."

All night, Little Wolf stays with Brave Bear.
The two boys sleep in the woods.
In the moon-filled quiet woods.

Now it is the morning of the next day.
The sun begins to rise.
The sun rises higher and higher in the sky.
The sun shines on the two boys
who are going home.

Brave Bear goes home with Little Wolf.
He tells Hunt Wolf and Flower Wolf and
Wise Wolf what has happened in the woods.

Hunt Wolf says,
"I am glad you are well, Brave Bear.
Our tribe needs you.
You will be a mighty hunter some day."

Then Hunt Wolf looks at his son and smiles.
"Our tribe needs you, too, Little Wolf.
You will be a mighty healer some day."
And Wise Wolf nods his head.

This day Flower Wolf will cook.
Hunt Wolf will hunt.
Wise Wolf will sit by the fire.
And Little Wolf,
Little Wolf will go to the woods.

He will not kill the deer or the rabbit or the fox.
He will see the animals
that run through the woods.
He will watch them.
And he will learn.

He will see the plants that grow in the woods.
He will study them.
And he will learn.

And that is Little Wolf's way.

Ann McGovern

18

Robert, Who Is Often
A Stranger to Himself

Do you ever look in the looking-glass
And see a stranger there?
A child you know and do not know,
Wearing what you wear?

Gwendolyn Brooks

Lonely Maria

Maria lived with her family on a small island in the West Indies. Her father was a fisherman. Every day he went out in his boat with his fish traps. Her mother was busy doing work near their house.

At night as Maria lay in bed she could hear the leaves rustling as though they were whispering together, but she could never understand what they said.

Maria's grandfather was an old man.

Every fine day he sat outside their house, sometimes in the sun, sometimes in the shade. He was always busy making or mending fish nets.

No other children lived near Maria. The sea was her best friend.

It talked with Maria, and at night it sang her to sleep. It sent its waves along the shore to play games with her. It brought her gifts of shells. And it gave her the sandy beach all for her own.

21

Maria loved the beach. She often sat there and drew pictures in the sand with a stick. She was like her grandfather. She could make things with her hands.

But one day she grew tired of all her games.

She went to her grandfather.

"Grandfather," she said, "I am lonely."

Her grandfather sat and for a long time he looked out across the sea.

Then he said, "I, too, used to be lonely when I went fishing all alone in my boat. But at last I learned that I could make anything happen. I remember how one day my little boat was surrounded by mermaids, all playing music."

"How did you do it, Grandfather?" Maria asked.

"Everyone must find his own way," said her grandfather.

So Maria went back to her beach and thought and thought and thought, and at last she picked up a stick and drew a picture of a house in the sand.

Thinking of the house, Maria closed her eyes, and when she opened them, a wonderful thing had happened. There stood the house and she could go into it whenever she liked.

Now the next day, Maria thought that she would like a garden, so she took her stick and drew flowers in the sand. And when she had closed her eyes, up sprang all sorts of beautiful flowers, filling the air with their sweetness.

But when Maria's father came back from his fishing, he walked past her new house and right through her garden and never saw them.

The very next morning, Maria drew a goat in the sand. No sooner had she closed and opened her eyes than the goat bleated. She was as white as the foam of the sea, so Maria named her Blanca.

Now came a day when the wind began to blow and clouds appeared over the sea. Maria knew that a storm would come soon. Quickly she took her stick and drew a horse in the sand, and when she opened her eyes, the horse neighed. He was gray and white like the clouds over the sea, and Maria named him Pinto.

Then Maria climbed on Pinto's back and with Blanca following, she raced across the island. She raced right past her own house, but neither her mother at the window, nor her grandfather mending nets by the open door, saw her go by.

The next day the sea was fierce and Maria's father did not go fishing. When Maria put a shawl over her head to go out, her mother said, "It is too windy, Maria."

"I will be gone only a little tiny minute," promised Maria.

The waves and wind were very noisy, but Maria, holding tight to the blowing shawl, ran down to see her house and garden and Blanca and Pinto.

"Be careful of them," she said to the waves, and ran back to her house fast, fast, with the wind behind her.

Soon after, came the rain.

All that day the wind and rain howled across the island, tearing at the palm leaf roof of the house. Fiercely the waves threw themselves far up the shores. But early next morning, when Maria woke, the storm was over and the sun was shining again.

Maria crept out of the house on tiptoe so as not to disturb the others.

But when Maria came to the beach, she found no house, no garden, no Blanca, no Pinto! The storm had washed them all away.

Maria thought that her heart would break. For a long, long time she ran up and down the beach looking and calling for her lost friends. But at last Maria knew that it was no use. The sea had taken them away.

What should she do? Maria turned to go home. But no. That would not help. She came slowly back to the beach. The storm had uprooted a tree. Maria sat down on the smooth trunk and thought and thought.

For a long time she sat there, looking out at the sea.

Then suddenly Maria jumped up. She had made up her mind what to do. Only Maria could help Maria now. She ran along the beach until she found a stick. Then she drew something very fast in the sand. She was frowning. Once or twice she rubbed out what she had drawn with one foot, and drew it over again.

When Maria had finished, she stood looking at her picture and shook her head. She added something and looked again. Then at last she gave a little nod. It would have to do.

Maria closed her eyes, and when she opened them what in the wide world do you suppose she saw standing there on the beach, very large and very gentle?

It was an elephant!

Perhaps the elephant wasn't quite like other elephants. Maria had seen a picture of an elephant named Jumbo in one of her mother's old school books, but she had not looked at it carefully.

Still, he was very large and grand. And he *was* an elephant. From the moment she laid eyes on him, Maria loved him. She named him Jumbo.

Jumbo knew how to act like an elephant. He knelt down and with his trunk lifted Maria and put her on his head.

From her high seat Maria looked down at her great friend, the sea, and smiled.

"You can take everything away from me, if you want to. I'll be unhappy but I'll start right over again," she said. "If you take Jumbo, I'll make a giraffe with a red saddle, and if someday you take my giraffe, I'll," she stopped to think of the most wonderful creature she could think of, and then said, all in a rush, "I'll make a gentle dragon and ride *him!* I'll always be able to make *something* wonderful, whatever you do!"

And calling goodbye to the sea, Maria rode off, while all the waves stood on tiptoe to watch her go and waved their white caps gaily.

Elizabeth Coatsworth

31

End
Of
the Line

Cary was very lucky. She had a grandfather who had all the time in the world to do things and go places just with her. They took long walks and visited the library, the parks and the zoo.

But of all the things they did, there were two things that they liked to do the best. Cary and her grandfather loved to go fishing. And they loved to ride on the old streetcars.

Although they almost never caught a fish, at least once a week they packed a good big lunch and off they went with their fishing poles and tackle box. There was a certain old pier which was their favorite place to go fishing.

On other days they rode all over town on the rusty, dusty creaking old streetcars. Cary's grandfather had once been a streetcar conductor and ever after rode free on the streetcars.

All the conductors were their friends. They always greeted each other with a "Hi, Charley!" and "How you been, Tom?" "How-do, Cary. Climb aboard!"

Cary and her grandfather were sometimes the only people on the streetcar because, more and more, people rode the new buses that whizzed past the old streetcars. Why this should be, Cary could never understand. She thought that a streetcar was worth a couple of buses anytime.

One day after they had been fishing all afternoon, Cary and her grandfather walked up from the beach to the corner where they waited for the streetcar.

"Humph," Cary heard Grandfather say, more to himself than to her. "Won't be any natural resources left around here. Nothing but people."

Cary was very curious. "Natural resources?" she asked.

"Oh," said Grandfather, "fish and wild animals and trees—those are natural resources. Take fish. There's no fish living around that pier anymore. And I think I know the reason."

"Why?" asked Cary, sitting beside him on the bench. She was watching the way the sunset was turning the street and the shops pink.

"The ocean floor is flat and sandy. Nothing at all left to make the fish want to swim there. No shelter of any kind. There needs to be something a fish can make a home in before he'll stay around. About the same as people, I guess. Well, here's Tom! A couple of minutes slow today, Tom!" called Grandfather, waving his tackle box.

He and Cary climbed up onto the big old streetcar.

Tom only nodded to them while he made change for someone else.

"What's the matter?" Grandfather asked him. "You look kind of glum." He offered Tom a lemon drop.

Tom shook his head.

"Haven't you heard the news?" he asked sadly.

"What news?" asked Cary's grandfather.

"They're going to scrap the streetcars, Henry!"

"Scrap the streetcars?" asked Cary and her grandfather.

"You heard me," said Tom, clanging the old streetcar's bell fiercely. "The city's going to turn 'em into junk. Every last one of them! It's the end of the line for the streetcars."

That night Cary had a strange dream. Like most dreams it was mixed up, but mostly it had to do with a family of fish—all dressed up like people and getting on a streetcar!

The next morning Cary laughed when she remembered the dream. She lay in bed for a while thinking about it. Suddenly she jumped out of bed and ran down the hall to Grandfather's door.

"Grandfather!" she shouted. "Are you awake? I've got a wonderful idea!"

She knocked on the door. "It's about the streetcars, Grandfather. Get up. We've got to go down to see the mayor."

Grandfather opened his door. "The streetcars, Cary? What's your idea?"

That very morning Cary and Grandfather went down to see the mayor. But they had to wait and wait a long everlasting wait to see him.

"Mayor Olson will see you now," the person at the desk finally said.

"What can I do for you?" asked the mayor.

"It's about the streetcars," said Cary.

"Yes, young lady?" said the mayor. "They're going to be scrapped, you know."

"Yes, sir, we know," said Cary. "And my grandfather and I don't think that that's the right thing to do at all."

"Is that so?" asked the mayor. "Well, I tell you, nobody ever rides them anymore. We've got fine buses in our city. The streetcars aren't good for anything but junk now."

"We think they could be good for something," said Cary. "We think the streetcars could increase the natural resources here around Oldport."

"Increase the natural resources?" asked the mayor. "Streetcars?"

"Yes," said Cary.

"What natural resource?" asked the mayor.

"More fish," said Cary.

Early one morning two weeks later the lighthouse keeper in Oldport Bay stuck his head out the window. Then he rubbed his eyes. "What's going on?" he wondered.

Cary and her grandfather stood on their favorite pier. A crowd had also gathered to watch the U.S. Navy and men from the Fish and Game Department hard at work. They were lowering the streetcars of Oldport into the bay!

"Now that's more fitting," said Grandfather.

Just then the mayor walked out to them on the pier.

"That was a mighty fine idea that your granddaughter had," he said. "As soon as I found from the Fish and Game Department that making shelter has been found to increase the number of fish I got busy. They said that streetcars, with all those windows to go in and out of, you know, would be perfect. Even got the Navy to help," he added with pride. "Well, there goes the last one down."

Cary was wondering what the fish would think. She pictured them nosing in and out of the cars that had carried people for so many years.

"Wait a minute," said Grandfather suddenly. "Did you say that's the last one they're lowering now?"

41

"I did," said the Mayor.

"Well, it's not!" said Grandfather firmly. "That's five that've gone down to the fish. How about old Number Six?"

The mayor's eyes twinkled. "Get in my car. I've something to show you."

Cary and Grandfather rode uptown with the mayor. There they found old Number Six. It had a new coat of paint and was standing near the middle of the park, not far from the library.

"What's the sign over the door there say, Cary?" asked Grandfather.

"Why, the sign says 'Streetcar Conductors' Clubhouse,' " said Cary. "And look, Grandfather, they are planting flowers and shrubs all around it."

"Well, Mayor," said Mr. Michael. "This is a fine thing. Wait till I tell Tom and Charley!"

We're planning a little party tonight," said the mayor. "The band will play and there will be food. Would you make a little speech, Mr. Michael? Something about the history of the streetcars?"

"Yes, I will be happy to," said Grandfather proudly. "There's no one who knows more about them."

That evening under a big moon the city park, gay with party lights, was filled with people. Everybody came for the opening of the Retired Streetcar Conductors' Clubhouse.

While Grandfather made his streetcar speech, Cary sat on the front row beside her mother and father and all the old streetcar conductors.

And ever after that, the streetcar clubhouse was a cheery place for people to meet and chat a while whenever they were downtown. On cold days it was always a good place to get warm around the little stove, and there were always plenty of apples and lemon drops. And in the summer, the Oldport pier became famous for the many, many fish that lived in the waters of Oldport Bay.

Janice May Udry

Lemons and Apples

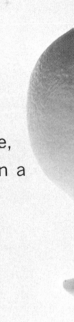

One day I might feel
Mean,
And squinched up inside,
Like a mouth sucking on a
Lemon.

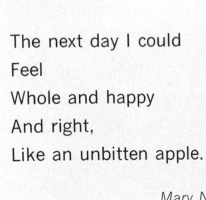

The next day I could
Feel
Whole and happy
And right,
Like an unbitten apple.

Mary Neville

45

The Fastest Quitter in Town

The pitcher threw the ball to home plate. Crack! The batter hit a grounder. The shortstop scooped it up. He threw it to Johnny Colmer.

"Easy out, Johnny," he yelled. Johnny touched one foot on first base, ready to make the catch. He knew he had it! But the only thing he caught was . . . air!

Johnny threw down his mitt. "I quit," he said. Everybody started yelling.

"You always quit when you do something stupid!"

"Why don't you learn to catch?"

Johnny yelled back. "I *can* catch. Old Gromering can't throw."

"Come on. Let's play without him. We don't need him," the boys said.

Johnny picked up his mitt and ran off the field. When he got to the edge of the school yard, he sat down on the curb. He felt awful. He had promised himself that he would play the whole game today. But he had quit right at the start.

Johnny got up and wiped his face on his shirt. He decided to go see Great-Grandfather and tell him about Gromering's bad throw. Johnny Colmer lived with his mother and father. His grandparents lived next door. But someone else lived there, too—Johnny's great-grandfather, who was ninety years old.

Great-Grandfather could hardly see anything. But he had lots of good stories to tell. He told Johnny about the first cars, and about days when there was no TV.

When Johnny arrived, the first thing Great-Grandfather said was, "Short game today?"

Johnny put his hands in his pockets. He didn't say anything.

"I thought you were going to play the whole game today. Something go wrong?" asked Great-Grandfather.

"Yeah," said Johnny.

"I see," Great-Grandfather said. "Well, do you suppose your grandmother has any cookies hidden away from us?"

Johnny reached for the cookies. "Fig newtons," he said.

"Oh, no!" said Great-Grandfather.

"I like them," Johnny said.

"Well, don't save any for me," said Great-Grandfather.

Johnny ate five fig newtons.

"Get yourself some milk," Great-Grandfather said. "Then tell me about today. Someone break the rules?"

"No," Johnny said. "Just Joe Gromering. He thinks he's so hot. Only he never learned to throw a ball."

"That's why you quit? You missed the ball?"

"Not exactly. I mean, kind of. Well, tomorrow I'm going to play the whole game no matter what those stupid guys do."

Great-Grandfather patted him on the back. "Tomorrow you'll catch the ball. But Johnny, if by some chance you miss it, don't give up. Keep playing. It's a game. You're supposed to have fun."

The next afternoon Johnny walked over to the school yard.

"Oh, no," the boys groaned. "Here comes Colmer, the fastest quitter in town."

Johnny stood around just hitting his mitt while the other boys played.

Finally one boy called, "All right, Colmer. We'll give you one more chance. Are you going to play the whole game today?"

"Yeah," said Johnny.

"O.K. Get out in left field."

In the third inning, when Johnny went to bat, he hit the ball far into center field. It looked like a homer. He ran fast. As he turned third base, he saw the ball moving toward the catcher.

"Slide!" someone yelled. He slid! He got up smiling and brushed the dirt off his torn pants. He was sure he was safe.

"Out!" yelled everyone.

"I'm safe!" Johnny shouted.

"You're out!" they yelled.

Johnny tried not to say anything, but suddenly the words came out. "I quit."

Everybody began to scream and yell. "That was your last chance, Colmer. You're off the team for good. Don't come around ever again," they said.

Johnny went straight to see Great-Grandfather. But he didn't tell him about the game because the old man was very upset.

"What's the matter, Great-Grandpa?" Johnny asked.

"Oh, Johnny," the old man said, "thank goodness you've come. I need your eyes, Johnny. You know my ring, the gold one with the real diamond in the center? The one your great-grandmother gave me? You never knew her. She died before you were born. I've lost the ring she gave me."

"Where did you lose it, Great-Grandpa? I'll find it," said Johnny.

Johnny crawled under Great-Grandfather's bed. He looked through Great-Grandfather's pillowcase and sheets and blankets to see if the ring had fallen off his finger while he slept. He pulled up the pillow on his favorite chair. He put his fingers in the cracks to see if the ring had fallen in there. He looked everywhere. But he couldn't find it.

Johnny looked for the ring every day for a week. But he did not find it.

"I've got to find that ring, Johnny. I promised I'd never take it off. And now I've lost it."

"It must have fallen off. You can't help that," Johnny said.

Each day the old man got more disturbed.

"Great-Grandpa," Johnny said, "I promise if your ring can be found, I will find it. I will never stop looking. I will never give up."

"Do you mean that, Johnny? Do you mean you won't quit on me?"

For almost a month, Johnny didn't go near the school yard when the boys were playing ball. He was busy with his promise to Great-Grandfather. He looked and looked. Each day when he woke up, he always felt it would be the special day when he would find the ring. But it never was.

One day when Johnny went to see Great-Grandfather, the old man said, "Johnny, I feel like a little sun. Help me out to the porch, will you?"

They sat on the porch together. The sun felt good on the old man's hands.

"You haven't stopped looking, have you, Johnny? I've got to have that ring."

"Great-Grandpa, I'll find it. Really, I'll find it!"

Johnny looked at the back yard. "Great-Grandpa, were you out back here on the day you lost your ring?"

The old man bent his head to one side. "I don't know. It's so hard to remember any more."

"Maybe you were. I've looked everywhere else." Johnny got down and crawled around the grass.

"Johnny, sometimes when I'm out here, I walk over to touch the flowers. I can't see them too well, but I like to touch them. Look over there, Johnny."

Johnny crawled through the grass looking. He came to the flowers and touched the earth around their stems. He separated the red ones from the yellow ones and looked through their leaves. He saw something near a flower stem—something shiny. Something gold sparkled in the sunlight.

"Great-Grandpa!" he yelled. "I found it!" He took the ring to his great-grandfather. Tears came to the old man's eyes. He felt the lost ring. There was dirt caked on the little diamond.

"He found my ring! Johnny found my diamond ring! Thank you, Johnny. I don't know what I would have done without you."

The whole family was thrilled. Johnny's grandmother put tape around the ring so it would not fall off again. Johnny felt so good inside. It was such a good feeling to have found the ring. He hadn't given up. He hadn't even wanted to quit. The ring meant so much to Great-Grandfather, he *never* would have quit.

The next day he went around to the school yard. The boys all laughed when they saw him.

"Well, look who's here," they said. "Long time, no see."

"How about one more chance?" Johnny asked. The boys hooted and laughed.

"For Colmer, the quitter?" they said.

The boy at bat called, "He was kicked out for good."

Other boys shouted, "No! He's a quitter."

But Gromering yelled, "C'mon, you guys. You know we need another player. Get over on third base, Johnny."

Johnny ran to third before they could change their minds.

It was after supper when he dropped in to see Great-Grandfather.

Great-Grandfather said, "It's late. You came late today. Where have you been?"

Johnny looked at his great-grandfather. He reached over and touched the lines in the old man's face. They were so deep. They kept getting deeper and deeper.

"Can't you guess why I'm late, Great-Grandpa? I was playing baseball. I used to be a quitter! But today I didn't quit. And I feel great."

"You a quitter?" Great-Grandfather asked. "That can't be. Not my Johnny. Did you win? I sure hope you won, Johnny."

"No, we lost," Johnny said. "Boy, did we ever lose! Twenty to seven. But I got two home runs! I don't know what the team would have done without me."

"I wish I could have seen you make those home runs."

Johnny helped the old man into the kitchen. They ate the cookies that Johnny's grandmother had made that day.

"Well, I'm so tired. I better get to bed," Great-Grandfather said.

Johnny helped him back to his room. "Goodnight, Great-Grandpa," Johnny said. "And thanks. Thanks a lot."

"Don't thank me," Great-Grandfather said. "Your grandmother made the cookies. See you tomorrow."

Phyllis Green

Friends with Nature

Little Wolf learned that herbs and plants he found in the forest could cure sick people. Maria learned that the sand and the sea could be companions for her when she was lonely. In "End of the Line" Cary discovered how to make fish come back to her favorite fishing spot. Each of these characters discovered how nature could be his or her friend.

What are some of the things in nature that you could become friends with? Pick one or two of your favorites, and explain *how* you would become friends with them. Would you watch them? Or listen to them? Or touch them? Here are a few to choose from, but you will probably think of many others.

butterflies
the rain
mountains
the wind
flowers
the stars
trees
chipmunks

Fancy That

Dooly
and the
Snortsnoot

There was once a family of giants.

The father giant was taller than a two-story building.

The mother giant was that tall too.

And they had a son, named Dooly, who wasn't any bigger than you.

Now, while your size is just right for YOU, it's a bit small for a giant. Dooly's mother and father worried about him.

Mother said, "Eat your vegetables, Dooly, so you'll grow big and strong like me and your father."

But it was plain to see that it was going to take an awful lot of vegetables.

Dooly did as he was told, but nothing seemed to help. He never got any bigger.

"I'll always be little!" said Dooly, and he started to cry.

"Little or big, you're still a giant," Father reminded him. "And giants don't cry. Giants are brave."

It's hard to be brave when you're not very big. But Father was right. Dooly was a giant, whatever his size.

One of the things that giants do is say, "FEE FI FO FUM!" at people and scare them half out of their wits. This makes the giant feel important. And when you feel important, you feel big.

65

So one day Dooly went into the village to scare somebody.

The first person Dooly saw was a girl named Treena.

Dooly stood on tiptoe to make himself as tall as he could, made a scowly face, and said, "FEE FI FO FUM!"

Treena giggled.

"I'm a GIANT!" Dooly declared.

"Not a very scary one," said Treena. Then, quite suddenly, she shouted, "FEE FI FO FUM!"

Dooly was so startled he jumped a foot.

"THAT'S the way to do it!" said Treena.

Some other children came over to ask what was going on.

"We're being giants," Treena explained.

So all the children, who had been wondering what to play next anyway, went around on their tiptoes saying, "FEE FI FO FUM!" And Dooly had to admit that most of them did it better than he could.

After a while they got tired of being giants and began to play tag. Dooly was "it" most of the time.

Dooly went into the village and played with the other children quite often after that.

He liked being with them, but he wasn't very good at their games.

When they played baseball, he was first one out.

When they ran a race, he was last one in.

And when they played hide-and-go-seek, Dooly was always the first one found.

He did the best he could, though. And it was fun, even if he didn't ever win.

But every once in a while Dooly would remember that he was a giant. And giants like to feel important. So he would say, "FEE FI FO FUM!"

The children would look up from their games and say, "Not bad, Dooly. Keep trying. Who wants to play blindman's buff?"

But Dooly couldn't help being sad.

One day their play was interrupted by an awful snarling and snorting.

From around the corner came the Terrible Snarly Snortsnoot, who eats little children for lunch! He was gnashing his teeth and thrashing his tail and breathing fire! He was a terrible sight to see.

The children turned and ran, with the Snortsnoot snarling at their heels.

But the Snortsnoot had decided he wanted to have Treena for lunch.

And with two snorts and a snarl he leaped and caught her.

He licked his lips and got ready to eat her.

"We've got to get Treena!" shouted Dooly.

"How CAN we?" asked the other children, quivering with fear.

Dooly didn't know. He was just as frightened as they were. But he ran toward the Snortsnoot, determined to do the best he could.

He looked at the Snortsnoot's fierce claws and shivered.

He looked at the Snortsnoot's wicked teeth and trembled.

And THEN he took a deep breath and stomped on the monster's tail.

The Snortsnoot gave a bellow and dropped Treena.

He scowled a terrible scowl and he growled a terrible growl as he turned and went after Dooly. One lunch was as good as another. He'd eat Dooly instead of Treena.

Dooly started to run. But then he remembered that he was a giant. And giants are brave. Giants don't run from Snortsnoots, no matter how snarly.

So Dooly stopped running and stood still.

The Snortsnoot opened his mouth to gobble Dooly whole.

Then all of a sudden Dooly said, "FEE FI FO FUM!" right in the monster's face. He said it just the way Treena had taught him.

The Snortsnoot was so surprised he forgot to gobble.

Then he remembered and opened his mouth again to swallow Dooly.

But something strange had happened. Dooly had grown almost a foot taller.

"So much the better," thought the Snortsnoot. "He'll make a bigger lunch for me." And the Snortsnoot opened his mouth wider.

"FEE FI FO FUM!" said Dooly again. And he grew another foot.

The Snortsnoot opened his mouth as wide as he could. But Dooly was growing too fast.

"FEE!" said Dooly and grew three feet.

"FI!" said Dooly and grew four more.

"FO!" said Dooly, and there was no longer any question that Dooly was a giant.

By the time he reached "FUM!" Dooly was so big he could have swallowed the Snortsnoot.

The Snortsnoot, who wasn't feeling very snarly anymore or hungry either, turned and ran and was never heard of again.

Nobody knew for sure what made Dooly grow.

His father said it was because he ate his vegetables, and no doubt that helped.

"I think," said Dooly's mother, "it was because he did a very big thing."

"I think I just grew up because it was time to," said Dooly modestly.

Jack Kent

The Thief Who
Hugged a Moonbeam

Once upon a time, long ago, there was a very greedy and successful thief. He had robbed many people and never been caught.

Swelled with confidence, the thief decided to break into the house of the richest man in the city.

He waited until it was almost dark. Then he climbed up to the roof of the rich man's house.

The thief tiptoed around, looking for a way to get in.

He bent over and listened to find out if anyone was at home.

The rich man heard him. "Aha," he thought. "A thief! Well, I'll play a good trick on him."

The rich man went to his wife. "There's a thief on the roof," he said, "but I have a plan. Come upstairs and ask me in a loud voice how I became so rich."

The woman was puzzled, but knowing this was no time for questions, she agreed.

"Tell me," she shouted, "how did you become so rich? I never saw you buy, sell, or cheat. Do tell me."

And the rich man told her this story, while the thief listened to every word.

"When I was young, I was a THIEF," said the rich man. "That is how I became so wealthy."

"But," interrupted his wife, "no one ever caught you or accused you of stealing. How is that?"

"My master," continued the rich man, "was a very wise and experienced old thief. It was he who taught me the magic word!"

"Magic word for what?" she asked.

"For hugging a moonbeam," said the rich man.

"I followed my master's instructions, and said the magic word seven times. Then I hugged a moonbeam and slid into the house I wanted to rob.

"When I had taken all that I could carry, I said the magic word seven more times. I hugged the moonbeam again, and was whisked silently and safely out of the house."

"What is the magic word?" asked the woman.

"It is very simple," said the rich man. "The word is *Sawool!*"

He repeated it even louder to make sure the thief heard. *"SAWOOL!"*

The couple went to bed. Pretending to sleep, they began to snore.

The thief heard their snores and thought it was safe now to enter the house.

"With the magic word, I will soon be as rich as the rich man!" the thief exclaimed.

Seven times he said "Sawool!" Then he stepped to the very edge of the roof, and wrapped his arms around a moonbeam.

And he fell straight down, grabbing a stovepipe here, a shutter there, and reaching wildly for a lamppost.

But there was nothing to stop his fall, and he landed with a loud splash in a rain barrel.

The rich man and his wife hurried downstairs.

Hearing the splash, all the neighbors came running.

The guards arrived and pulled the thief out of the rain barrel.

As they led him away, he could be heard mumbling . . . "But I said *Sawool* seven times. I said *Sawool* seven times. I said . . ."

The rich man called after him, "You should know better than to believe everything you hear, my man!"

"*Sawool!*"

Harold Berson

The Talking Tiger

If a tiger
Walks beside you
And he whispers:
"Where are you going?"
Do not answer,
Just keep walking
Just keep walking, walking, walking.
And if he continues talking
You keep walking.
Let him talk.
You just walk.
A talking tiger
Never bites,
A walking tiger
Never fights.
But if you find
That he's a bore
Then go right home
And shut the door.

Arnold Spilka

82

If You Ever Meet A Whale

If you ever, ever, ever, ever,
   ever meet a whale,
You must never, never, never, never
   grab him by his tail.
If you ever, ever, ever, ever,
   grab him by his tail—
You will never, never, never, never
   meet another whale!

Anonymous Rhyme

The Strange Story of the Frog Who Became a Prince

Many years ago there was a handsome frog who lived by a rather nice pond.

He had fun all day and at night he had happy dreams. Every day was exactly the same as every other day.

He liked to swim in the pond and hop in the grass. He hopped high and he hopped low. When he was feeling silly he hopped from side to side.

In the grass and in the pond the handsome frog found caterpillars, grasshoppers, and many other good things to eat.

His skin was green like the grass and brown like the pond and gold like the sun. He had black eyes which poked out on either side of his head.

He was a very handsome frog indeed.

One day he was minding his own business, catching caterpillars and doing some rather fine hopping when a wicked witch came swimming across the pond. She had a wet black hat and a wet black dress and she had black eyes right on the front of her face. She looked like a bad dream.

But the handsome frog thought she looked rather interesting.

"Will you join me for a lunch of caterpillar?" he asked the wicked witch as he took a happy jump to one side. "I'd be happy to cut mine in half."

"ICK!" said the wicked witch, making a face.

"What did you say?" he asked.

"People don't eat caterpillars," she said, making a face. "ICK!"

The frog looked at the interesting witch who had a face like a bad dream. "What do people eat if they don't eat caterpillars?" he asked.

The witch put her hand into her big wet pocket and took out a very wet peanut butter sandwich.

"Have some of this," she said. "I'll share it with you. It's very good." She broke the sandwich in half and handed him a piece.

The frog bit into the sandwich. "ICK!" he said.

The wicked witch looked at the handsome frog. She smiled a wicked smile. Then she snapped her fingers and said:

ECNIRP!

which sounded like a hiccup but which is really PRINCE spelled backwards.

Instantly the handsome frog turned into a prince.

"What have you done to me?" he asked.

"I've changed you into a prince," she said. "Aren't I smart?"

"But why?" he asked.

"Because I wanted to," she said.

He looked at his pink skin and felt his big ears and the hair on his round head. "My skin is as smooth as a worm, and my ears are like leaves, and my head has grass growing on it!" he cried. "Please change me back into the handsome frog I used to be."

The wicked witch smiled. "Oh, I can't do that," she said. "I don't remember how."

"Why, oh why did you do such a thing?" the prince asked, weeping. "I was such a handsome happy frog and then along you came and turned me into an ugly prince."

The wicked witch said, "I wanted to see if I could still do magic. Many years ago I changed a handsome prince into an ugly frog. What a good trick *that* was! But he was unhappy too. People just don't like anything new. Did you ever hear of him?"

"Indeed I did," said the prince. "They say he cried all day and frightened the baby frogs with all that talk about witches. They say he was a very low hopper and a slow swimmer as well. When he disappeared everyone said he had been changed back into a prince. Now, how did you do *that?*"

The witch shrugged. "Who can remember? It was years and years ago."

"Try to remember," said the prince.

"It was all part of a magic spell I've forgotten."

The prince said, "What was that magic word you said when you changed me into a prince?"

"I said PRINCE backwards," she said. "Some magic spells work that way. You have to keep trying new words because some work and some don't, although I've never known why."

"Well, try saying that one again," said the prince.

"ECNIRP!" said the witch loudly.

Nothing happened.

"Try FROG backwards," said the prince.

"GORF!" said the witch.

"Try WATER."

"RETAW!"

"Try SUN."

"NUS!"

"Try GRASS."

"SSARG," she hissed.

The prince thought hard and then said softly, "Try MAGIC WORD."

"What a good idea," said the witch. "CIGAM DROW!!!"

Nothing happened.

The prince sat down in the tall grass and began to cry again, more loudly than before.

"Now stop that," said the witch. "I don't know if you know this, but ANYONE WOULD RATHER BE A PRINCE THAN A FROG."

"Really?" asked the prince. "Why?"

The witch thought hard for a moment and then she said, "Well, for one thing, you can have a name when you're a person. A name tells people who you are. Pick any name you like and it will be yours. How about a fine name like TOM?"

"TOM?" said the prince. "Is that a name? It sounds like something falling in the grass at night when it's dark."

"How about HARRY?" asked the witch.

"Is *that* a name?" asked the prince. "It sounds like a cricket calling."

"What about a princely French name like ALPHONSE?" asked the witch.

"It sounds like a beaver sneezing," said the prince.

"You really are hard to please," said the witch. "Look at your nice clothes. Clothes keep you warm and make you look nice."

"Warm!" said the prince. "My legs are strangling. I'm boiling. I can hardly jump."

"Only necks can strangle," said the witch. "Only water can boil. Only frogs and horses and grasshoppers jump around in that boring way. And," said the witch, "people can learn how to read." She took a wet newspaper out of her wet pocket.

"You see, these are words," she said. "Look, this word says 'pond'."

"Pond?" he said. "It doesn't look like a pond at all. It looks just like muddy hummingbird footprints."

"How old are you anyhow?" said the witch.

"I was born in the spring," said the frog.

"Well, no wonder," said the witch. "You can't learn to read until you're older. I'm very sorry, but I don't know how to break the spell," said the witch, a little crabby now. "You'll just have to learn to like being a prince. Come now, I'll teach you how to whistle and snap your fingers. Now *there* are two things no frog can do."

The witch whistled "Row, Row, Row Your Boat" for the prince.

The prince tried and tried, but he could not whistle.

"Why would anyone want to whistle or snap his fingers anyhow?" asked the prince.

"Whistling is a very useful trick," said the witch. "You can call your dog when you whistle."

"I hate dogs," said the prince.

"Well, never mind," said the witch. "I'll teach you how to snap your fingers."

The witch snapped her fingers.

And suddenly she remembered.

She remembered that she had not snapped her fingers when she said her magic words backwards.

She leaned closer to the poor unhappy prince, looked into his sad eyes, snapped her fingers, and said:

CIGAM DROW!

"I feel different!" said the prince.

"Why, look what I've done!" said the witch. "I've changed you into a beautiful princess!! How charming!"

"HOW EMBARRASSING!!" said the princess who used to be a prince who used to be a frog. "Keep trying, please. I think you're on the right track."

SSARG!

said the witch, snapping her fingers.

And the princess who used to be a prince who used to be a frog changed again.

"You're getting warmer," said the centaur who used to be a princess who used to be a prince who used to be a frog.

The witch snapped her fingers again and said:

NUS! RETAW!

The merman who used to be a centaur who used to be a princess who used to be a prince who used to be a frog said, "Almost, but not quite. Try again."

The witch snapped her fingers very loudly twice and cried:

GORF, GORF!

And the spell was broken.

The handsome frog was very happy. He looked at himself in the pond, and he hopped high and he hopped low. Then he hopped from side to side. He swam across the pond and back. He ate a caterpillar.

"If you change your mind and want to be a prince again, just call me," said the witch, as she put on her swimming goggles.

"Oh, no!" said the frog. "But if I meet someone else who would like to be changed into a prince, how do I find you?"

"Just whistle or snap your fingers, and I'll be there," said the witch, as she jumped into the pond and swam away.

The handsome frog laughed. He laughed and laughed until he was very tired. Then he sat down on a warm rock and told the whole story to a tree toad, who didn't believe it.

Elinor Lander Horwitz

DRAGON STEW

Once upon a time there was a kingdom ruled by a king who was so fat that his people called him King Chubby. He was so fond of food that he couldn't bear to be without it for very long.

Eating was his hobby. He began with a big breakfast at eight o'clock, had a light snack at ten, and a large lunch at twelve. Then he exercised by watching two tennis players, and since exercise made him hungry, he ate a small snack at about two in the afternoon.

At four, he had sandwiches and at seven in the evening he happily sat down to a royal banquet. There was one of these every evening, even if the king was the only one at the table.

Eating was so important to him that it affected everything he did. When he fell in love with a duchess from another kingdom, he told her that he would almost rather look at her than eat a whole roast pig. Needless to say, the duchess never spoke to him again.

His love of eating also got him in trouble in other ways. He was always losing his royal cooks. He just couldn't keep from telling them how to improve their cooking. He insisted on making changes in every dish. Since royal cooks are very proud, they resented this. Six cooks had already left the job.

One evening when the king entered the banquet hall and saw a sandwich on his plate, he knew what had happened.

"Oh, my," he sighed, "I see number seven has left!"

"Yes, your Majesty," replied one of the servants, "he said he could no longer cook for a king who kept changing all his recipes. And now there are no more royal cooks left! None of those you've had will ever come back, and all the others are cooking for other kings. I don't know how to find another cook. There just aren't any!"

The king looked worried for a moment, then brightened. "I know! A royal cook *is* a royal cook because he can make up unusual recipes. We'll have a contest, and the one who tells me the most unusual recipe can be the royal cook!"

The next day signs were put up throughout the kingdom inviting all cooks to enter the contest. There was great excitement. Every cook from every inn in the kingdom came rushing to the castle.

They formed a line which began at the back of the castle, wound around to the front, and crossed the bridge. They entered the gate, jammed the courtyard, went up the stairs, and flowed into the throne room where the king was interviewing them. In they came, bowing, smiling, and offering enough recipes to fill seven fat cookbooks or seventy fat kings.

But to each, King Chubby shook his head. "That's not unusual," he'd say, or "I've had that before."

While this was going on, a shabby young man came trudging up the road toward the castle. He had patched knees and elbows, and the feather in his worn hat was bent, but he had a merry grin, and he was whistling a gay tune. When he saw the long line of people, he asked a soldier, "What's going on?"

"The king's looking for a new royal cook," the soldier replied. "The cook with the most unusual recipe will get the job and will live in the palace off the best of the land!"

"Wouldn't that be wonderful!"

"Well, I don't know," said the soldier. "Cooks don't get along with the king. He tells 'em what to do, puts things in their pots—he all but does the cooking himself."

"You don't say?" said the young man, and he got into line.

"Oh, are you a cook?" asked the soldier.

"I'm just the sort of cook the king wants," he answered, "and I have the most unusual recipe he's ever heard of!"

It was late afternoon when he reached the throne room. The king was looking very glum. Not one cook had offered a recipe he thought was unusual. And now the last of them was this shabby fellow who looked far too thin to be much of a cook. "Well, what's your name and recipe?" he asked.

"I'm Klaus Dinkelspiel, your Majesty. My recipe is so unusual, so rare, that I'll bet you've never heard of it. It's—dragon stew!"

The king gasped. "That sounds different. What's in it—besides dragon, of course?"

"Oh, I can't tell you!" said Klaus. "It has been a secret in my family for hundreds of years."

"I understand," nodded the king, "but if we can ever locate a dragon, you must make it for me. However, you can begin preparing a royal banquet for tonight. You are the new royal cook."

Klaus bowed deeply. "And what would you like for dinner?" he asked.

"How about roast pig with applesauce?"

"And would your Majesty care to show me exactly how you want it cooked?" Klaus asked innocently.

The king stared. "You mean you won't care if I offer advice? Why, you and I are going to get along just fine!"

So off they went to the kitchen and got together everything the king needed. Then Klaus said, "Now, how would you prepare this, your Majesty?"

King Chubby, very pleased, stuffed the pig, tied it up, and then peeled and sliced the apples.

"How would you cook this, your Majesty?"

So the king happily popped the pig into the oven. He took turns stirring the applesauce and turning the pig.

Klaus watched and kept saying, "Just how I'd have done it."

When the pig was brown and savory and the sauce bubbling merrily, he said, "I thank you for all your help, sire. If you will go to the banquet hall, I'll serve you the banquet I have prepared."

When the king had gobbled up the last piece of pork and bit of sauce, he announced that it was the finest banquet he'd ever eaten and Klaus was the finest cook he'd ever had. And from then on, the king and his new cook were both pleased—King Chubby because he now had all his favorite dishes cooked exactly as he liked them and Klaus because he was living off the best of the land.

One morning, a good many months after Klaus had become the royal cook, he was called to the throne room. When he entered, he was shocked to see the Captain of the guard and a dozen scratched and smoke-blackened soldiers surrounding a large cage inside of which was a small, fat dragon.

"Surprise!" beamed the king. "I sent them out to find a dragon months ago, and it's taken all this time to find one. Now you can cook your special dragon stew tonight. I promise I won't try to find out your secret—I won't even set foot in the kitchen today!"

The soldiers carried the cage to the kitchen, set it down, and trooped out. The captain said, "Careful of him, Cook—he bites, scratches, and can shoot fire six inches out of his nose."

Klaus stared at the small dragon. A tear rolled down its cheek. "Are you trying to think of the best way to kill me?" it asked. "It isn't fair! I was minding my own business, bothering no one, and suddenly your soldiers attacked me and carried me here to be made into—into stew." He sniffled.

111

"Believe me, dragon," said Klaus, "I don't want to make you into stew. I didn't think there were any dragons when I made up that silly recipe. I just wanted to trick the king into thinking I was a cook. I couldn't make any stew if my life depended on it—and it probably does. The king will have me beheaded when he finds out that I tricked him."

"Oh, making a stew is easy," said the dragon. "You soak the meat in oil and spices, brown it in butter and simmer it slowly in broth with onions and carrots. I always throw in a few mushrooms and some parsley, too. And then . . ."

"You can cook?" interrupted Klaus. "I thought dragons only ate raw princesses and things like that."

"Heavens, no!" the dragon shuddered. "Really, I'm a good cook. Living alone, I've had to do all my own cooking. I've become quite a chef, if I do say so myself." He blew a smoke ring from his left nostril.

Suddenly, Klaus began to grin and nod his head as though he had thought of something.

At seven o'clock, the king hurried into the banquet hall, tingling to taste Klaus' wonderful dragon stew. He watched closely as Klaus carried in a steaming bowl and ladled chunks of beautifully browned meat and vegetables swimming in rich gravy onto the king's plate. King Chubby began to gobble. After four helpings, he leaned back with a sigh.

"That certainly is one of the best stews I've ever eaten. What a shame we can never have it again. That was probably the world's last dragon."

"Oh, we can have it as often as you like, your Majesty," Klaus calmly announced. "You see, the thing that makes dragon stew such a rare recipe is that it can only be cooked *by* a dragon! Allow me to present my assistant."

114

Klaus whistled, and in came the dragon, wearing a tall, white cook's hat and a gravy-stained apron. He bowed deeply.

"Under my direction," said Klaus with a charming grin, "my assistant will be happy to make dragon stew whenever you want it."

So everything turned out very well. King Chubby was able to cook his own banquets just as he liked them. He could also have dragon stew (made from beef) as often as he wanted it. Klaus was happy to be living off the best of the land without having to work hard for it. The dragon was very pleased to be an assistant royal cook.

But the happiest of all was the kitchen helper. One of his jobs had been to light the fire in the big stove, and he had always burned his knuckles. But now he no longer had this task, for the assistant cook lit his own stove by shooting fire out of his nose!

116

Tom McGowen

RUOK?

There are certain letters and numbers that sound like words. For example, *8* sounds like *ate* and *c* sounds like *sea*. Can you think of some others?

Try to read the sentences that go with each of the pictures below.

I M N D L-F-8-R

D L-F-N 8 D A

R U O K?
S, N-Q

R U C-P?
S, I M
I M 2

Now try reading some other sentences without the help of any pictures. When you understand each sentence, you might like to draw it.

D C-L S N D C
I C U
E S D 1 4 U 2 C
I M C-N U

117

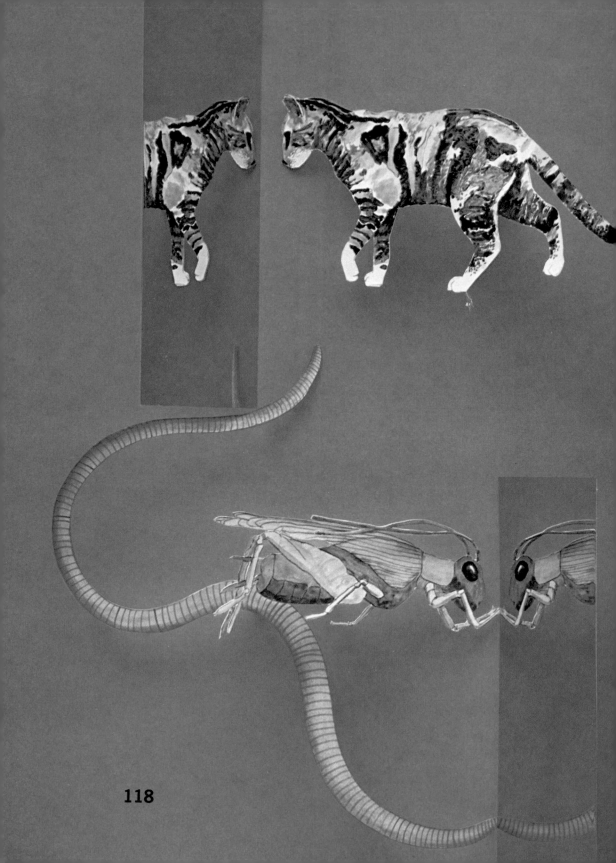

Creature Features

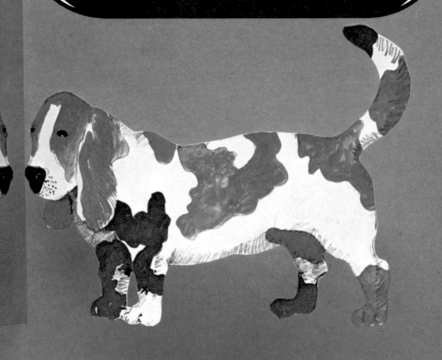

119

What Mary Jo Wanted

Every time Mary Jo saw a dog, any dog—big or little, black, white, old or young—she wished it belonged to her.

"I would rather have a dog than anything on earth," she said at least twice a week, usually at the dinner table. She sighed. "I'd be the happiest person in this town if I had a puppy." She often read the ads from the newspaper under "Pets for Sale" out loud to her parents.

"Puppies must be trained. It takes a lot of time," said her father.

"I'd love to train a puppy!" said Mary Jo. "I'd do it all myself!"

"Puppies cry at night when you first bring them home," said her father. "Nobody gets any sleep."

"They cry because they're lonesome. I'll be the one to get up in the night and talk to my puppy," said Mary Jo.

"They must be fed every day. They must have fresh water. They should be brushed. They must be given baths," said her father.

"I'd do it! I'd do it!" said Mary Jo. "I *want* to feed and brush and wash a dog."

121

"A good dog owner must take the full responsibility for her pet," said her father.

Responsibility was a word Mary Jo had heard a lot lately—ever since her sister had been given a canary for her birthday. She was being responsible for her bird, but she was quite a bit older than Mary Jo. Besides, a bird in a cage was not as great a responsibility as a puppy.

"I would be responsible," said Mary Jo.

Mary Jo read dog books by the dozen. She drew pictures of dogs. She wrote dog stories and dog poems. One morning she put a two-page theme by her father's plate, "Why I Want a Dog."

It looked as if fate were on Mary Jo's side when a new pet store opened downtown.

She showed the big opening day ad in the newspaper to her parents. She read: "Special for This Opening. Small, lovable puppies. Only $19 while they last!"

"I would like a badger," said Mary Jo's brother. "Do they have any badgers?" Jeff had just been looking at a picture of a badger family in a new book from the library.

"Can't we go down to see the new pet store? And the puppies?" Mary Jo begged.

"All right, Mary Jo. I believe you're old enough to take care of a puppy," said her father.

"Oh," shouted Mary Jo. "Get your coats, everybody! Let's go!"

"They *are* cute," said Mary Jo's mother when they stood gazing down at a little pen full of puppies in the new pet store.

"Cute!" said Mary Jo. "They're the sweetest creatures ever born in this world!"

Her father laughed. "Which one do you want?"

Mary Jo knew right away. One little furry baby had wobbled over to lick her fingers the minute she knelt beside the pen.

"This one," she said. "He came right to me. He's the most lovable!"

"Have him wrapped up then," said her father.

"Wrapped up?" said Mary Jo. Then she saw that her father was joking. He got out his billfold.

The first thing the family did when they got home was to put newspapers all over the kitchen floor.

"It's only until you're housebroken," she told him. He reached playfully for her shoe string and looked up into her face.

"Be sure to call the vet this week and make an appointment," said Mary Jo's father. "He should have his puppy shots right away."

Mary Jo and her friend Laurie spent hours deciding on a name for him. They made lists and pored over the section of names at the back of the dictionary.

Jeff suggested "Mr. Picklepone." That was the silliest name he could think of.

In the end they decided on "Teddy" because the puppy looked so much like a small teddy bear, and he even squeaked.

He squeaked and cried—*especially* at night. No matter how cozy Mary Jo made his bed in the kitchen or how many times Teddy yawned at bedtime, he always woke as soon as everyone was in bed and the house was still. He woke and cried as if his heart would break. Mary Jo put a night-light in the kitchen, in case he was afraid of the dark. She gave him a little snack at bedtime, in case he was hungry. She put an old toy dog in bed with him, hoping he would think it was another puppy. But he didn't.

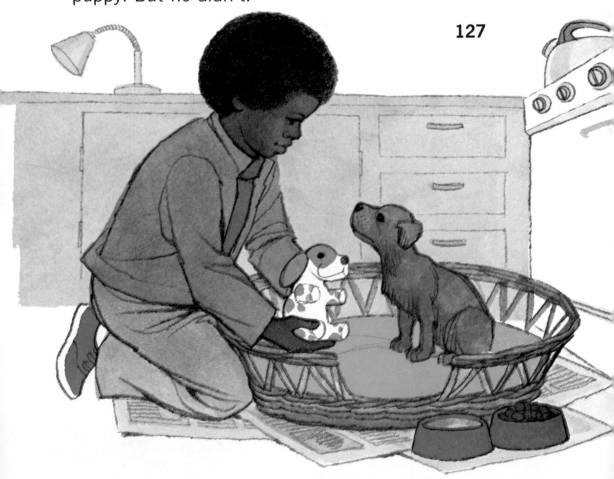

Mary Jo walked sleepily from her warm bed out to the kitchen a dozen times a night to see Teddy. As long as she was there, he was happy. He tried to get her to play as if it were the middle of the day instead of the middle of the night, and he licked her with his loving puppy tongue. As tired as she was, Mary Jo could never feel angry with him because he was so happy each time she appeared at the kitchen door.

But by the end of the first week she could hardly get up in the mornings. She was almost late for school. Everyone looked tired because although Mary Jo was the one who got up to soothe him, Teddy woke the others with his loud, sad little cries.

A neighbor told them to wrap a clock in a blanket and put that beside Teddy in the bed. "He'll hear the tick and think it's another puppy," she told them. But it didn't fool Teddy for one minute.

Finally one morning Mary Jo's mother found her asleep on the paper covered kitchen floor.

"Is this ever going to end?" Mary Jo's mother asked at the breakfast table. "I don't ever remember hearing of any puppy crying as many nights as this one has."

"Some of them get used to being alone faster than others I guess," said Mary Jo's father. "But I'm beginning to wish we had never seen that dog!"

"I'm responsible," thought Mary Jo. "I've *got* to think of something to keep Teddy quiet."

That afternoon when she went to the basement to get some old newspapers for the kitchen floor she saw something that gave her an idea.

After dinner that night Mary Jo said, "You'll be able to sleep tonight. I've thought of a way to keep Teddy quiet."

"What is it?" asked her mother.

"You'll see," said Mary Jo. She went down to the basement.

Her parents heard her lugging something up the stairs. It was an old folding cot.

"I'm going to sleep in the kitchen until Teddy is housebroken and can sleep in my room," she said.

Her mother and father looked at each other.

"Why not?" said her father. "That's probably the only thing that will solve the problem."

And it did. Teddy slept without making one squeak all night with Mary Jo on the old cot just above his basket.

Mary Jo thought it was fun to sleep in the kitchen. It was cozy to hear the clock hum and the faucet over the sink drip now and then. If she woke at daybreak, it was nice to see the new day arriving in the kitchen so early. There was a window to the east, so sunlight came to the kitchen first.

And it was fun to pretend to be asleep when her mother or father or brother came to the kitchen.

"Mary Jo, wake up!" they would say.

"Oh, is it morning already?" Mary Jo would say. "I was sound asleep."

And she hugged Teddy and tried not to giggle.

Janice May Udry

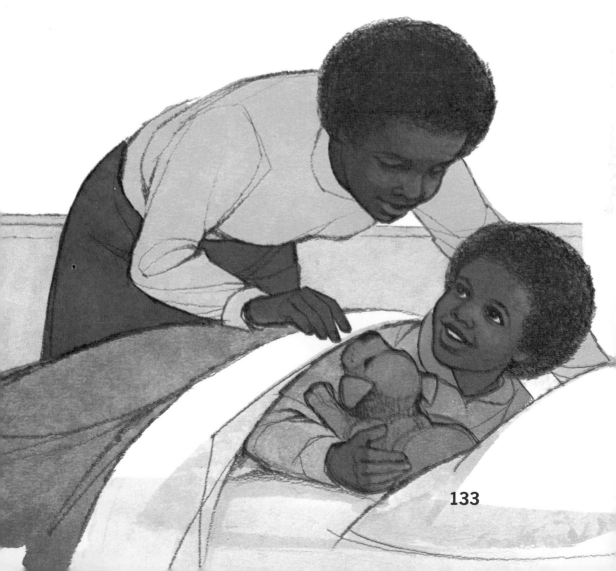

CAT

The black cat yawns,
Opens her jaws,
Stretches her legs,
And shows her claws.

Then she gets up
And stands on four
Long stiff legs
And yawns some more.

She shows her sharp teeth,
She stretches her lip,
Her slice of a tongue
Turns up at the tip.

Lifting herself
On her delicate toes,
She arches her back
As high as it goes.

She lets herself down
With particular care,
And pads away
With her tail in the air.

Mary Britton Miller

George

A dog went to live with a family. They did not go out and buy him. And he was not a gift from a friend. They did not find him. He found *them* and he moved in.

He was a big dog. And they were a big family. There was Ma. And Pa. And Grandma. And Grump. There was Alice. And little Anna May. And Willy. They were also a very busy family.

One day Grandma went out fishing in her little boat. And the big dog went along. He was not invited. He just went.

And he leaned too far over the side and the little boat turned over. Grandma lost her fishing rod and her oars and her oarlocks. She lost her bait and her bait box and she had to swim all the way home and she was simply furious.

"This dog must go!" she announced. But the rest of the family was too busy to pay much attention and the dog certainly did not pay any attention at all. Because he liked it there and it was his home.

That evening Grump read in the newspaper that there were to be many special big sales in the stores of a faraway town. The next morning he got up very early and put on his best clothes and jumped into his little car and drove all the many miles to the faraway town. Just when he arrived there and had the little car neatly parked, he heard a snoozing sound and he turned around and there was the big dog asleep on the back seat. He had not been invited. He just went.

Grump could not leave him locked in the car all day and he could not take him into the stores. All he could do was turn around and drive the long way home. He missed all the special big sales and he was simply furious.

"This dog must go!" he demanded. But the rest of the family was too busy to pay much attention and certainly the dog did not pay any attention at all. Because he liked it there and it was his home.

The next day Ma was late in getting ready to go to her office in the city. She had to run and jump onto the very last car of the train just as it was leaving. She hurried to her seat hearing everyone laugh as she went by. She looked down to see if she was still wearing her nightgown or had forgotten to put on her shoes. When she turned around to see if she was wearing her hat backwards she found out why they were laughing. Because there was the big dog paddling along close behind her. He had not been invited. He just went.

The conductor came and pulled the EMERGENCY rope and the train came to an emergency stop. Ma had to get off and walk the dog all the way home. She never did get to work at all that day and she was simply furious.

"This dog must go!" she stamped. But the rest of the family was too busy to pay much attention and the dog certainly did not pay any attention at all. Because he liked it there and it was his home.

The next day Pa invited some very important people to come and visit and stay for tea. And they came. Just when they were all standing on the sea wall looking at the view the big dog ran and leaped over them into the water to chase a clam or possibly a jellyfish or maybe a mermaid, and they all fell in.

Wearing their very best going-to-visit clothes they all fell in. That was the end of the tea party and the important people, and Pa was simply furious.

"This dog must go!" he stomped. But the rest of the family was too busy to pay much attention and certainly the dog did not pay any attention at all. Because he liked it there and it was his home.

The next day Alice started out on her paper route and the big dog tagged along. He was not invited. He just went.

She rode on her bicycle up one street and down the next, throwing the folded newspapers onto the porches of the houses on her route as she went by.

When she was all finished she rode home with the fine feeling of a hard day's work well done. But when she got there she found that the big dog had picked up all the papers that she had just delivered and carried them home to his own front door. So she had to gather them all up and start in on her paper route all over again and she was simply furious.

"This dog must go!" she steamed. But the rest of the family was too busy to pay much attention and certainly the dog did not pay any attention at all. Because he liked it there and it was his home.

The next morning Willy got up early to work in his flower garden. Willy had a beautiful garden. He had worked real hard all the hot summer to help the flowers grow tall and bloom full and bright. He planned to take them to the Fair in hopes that they would earn a prize ribbon there.

But he found that in the night the big dog had dug deep holes and buried big bones right in the middle of his best bed of mums—which is the quick way to say chrysanthemums. The dog had not been invited. He just dug. And now the long strong stems were broken and the little bright buds were squashed and Willy was simply furious.

"This dog must go!" he cried. But the rest of the family was too busy to pay much attention and certainly the dog did not pay any attention at all. Because he liked it there and it was his home.

The next day little Anna May went to the corner store. She took with her all her money that she had been saving for many weeks to buy a baseball and a catcher's mitt. The big dog went along. He was not invited. He just went.

He followed her into the store and there he gobbled up a big box of bonbons and he gobbled up a big box of chocolate cherries. He gobbled up a big box of jelly beans and he gobbled up a big box of gumdrops, and he galloped out of the store bigger than ever. Little Anna May had to use up all her money to pay for what he had eaten. She did not have any left to buy the baseball or the catcher's mitt and she was simply furious.

"This dog must go!" little Anna May sputtered. But the rest of the family was too busy to pay much attention and certainly the big dog did not pay any attention at all. Because he liked it there and it was his home.

And every day the big dog brought home kittens. One by one he carefully carried six kittens home from a neighbor's house because he just loved kittens. And every night the mother cat came to collect her kittens and while she was taking one back to her own home the big dog was bringing another one to *his* home and finally all the mother cat could do was to move in with the dog's family too and she was simply furious.

Also every Saturday he went to the town tennis courts and helped the people there play tennis, but they did not need his kind of help and they were simply furious.

Then on one very hot summer day nothing happened. The big dog did not tag along after anyone. He did not overturn any rowboat. He did not hide in an automobile. He did not climb aboard a railroad train. He did not push any important people into the water. Or any not important people either. He did not bury any bones in any garden. He did not carry home any newspapers. He did not gobble up any jelly beans or gumdrops. He did not carry home kittens or play tennis on the town tennis courts. He did not do anything. Because he was not there. He was gone.

And suddenly the big family felt simply lost without him. They got busy and began to look for him. They called and they whistled and they cried. They telephoned the town dog catcher. And the dog catchers of all the other towns around. They put an ad in the newspaper. They ran up one street and down the next. They rang doorbells and asked for him of everyone they met. They combed the countryside and searched the town. Everyone asked, "What is his name?" And then they were embarrassed when they had to answer that they had been just too busy to give him a name. And now they could not find the big dog anywhere. He was gone.

152

The neighbors helped in the search. And the people on the tennis court stopped their game and helped to look for him. And also the cat who was the mother of the big dog's kittens. She looked too. But no one could find him. He was gone.

At the end of that very hot day the big busy family gathered together at home to talk things over. They talked over what they had done and what they could do next.

The big dog, hearing their voices, woke from his sound sleep. He crawled out from under the cool back porch, where he had been all day. He yawned and stretched and yawned again. Then he crawled out of the deep cool hole he had dug in the dark earth under the porch.

He walked slowly into the house. They were all astonished to see him. Then they all rushed to greet him. Ma hugged him. And Pa squeezed him. And Grandma patted him. And Grump petted him. Alice cosied him. Little Anna May squoze him. And Willy kissed him. And they gave him a name. They named him George. And they all just love love love loved him.

The big dog did not know what all the fuss was about because he did not know that he had been lost. And the big family did not know he had *not* been lost, so they begged him not to be lost ever again.

The big dog did not understand their words, but of course he did know what they meant. They were saying what they were usually too busy to say. They were saying that they loved him, which of course he had always known. Because that was why he liked it there, and why it was his home.

Phyllis Rowand

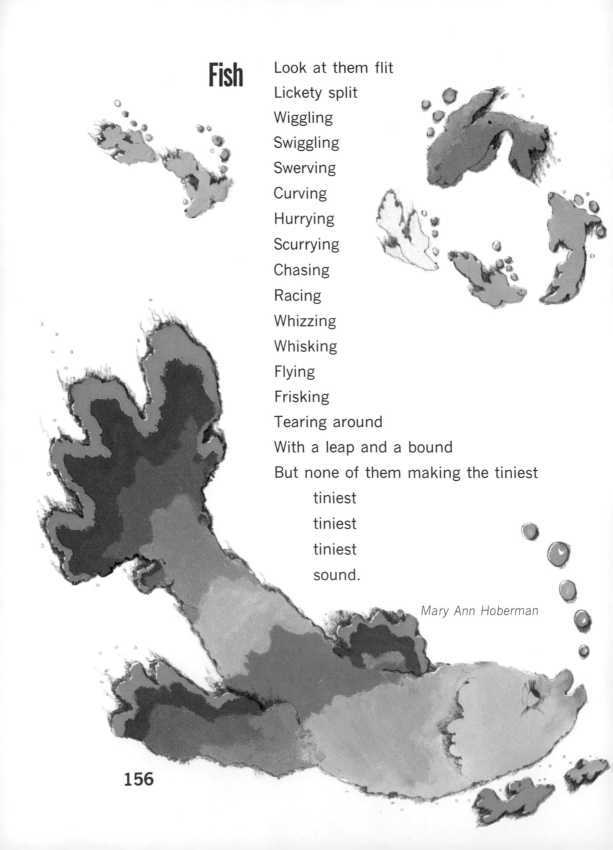

Fish

Look at them flit
Lickety split
Wiggling
Swiggling
Swerving
Curving
Hurrying
Scurrying
Chasing
Racing
Whizzing
Whisking
Flying
Frisking
Tearing around
With a leap and a bound
But none of them making the tiniest
    tiniest
    tiniest
    tiniest
    sound.

Mary Ann Hoberman

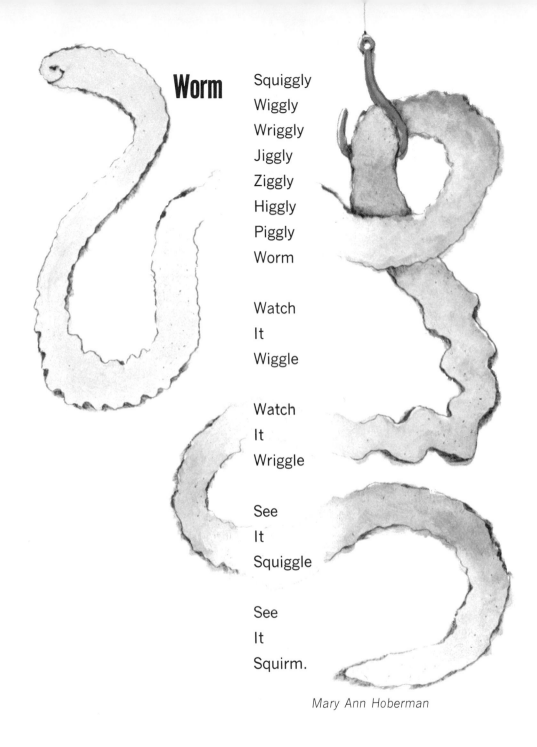

Worm

Squiggly
Wiggly
Wriggly
Jiggly
Ziggly
Higgly
Piggly
Worm

Watch
It
Wiggle

Watch
It
Wriggle

See
It
Squiggle

See
It
Squirm.

Mary Ann Hoberman

157

A Pocketful of Cricket

Part 1

This boy, Jay, lived with his father and his mother in an old farmhouse in a hollow.

All around his house Jay could see hills. He could see hills when he stood in the kitchen doorway. He could see hills when he swung on the gate in front of his house. When he climbed into the apple tree beside his house, he could see hills.

Woods covered most of the hills. Corn grew on some of them. On a far green hill, farther than Jay could see, cows ate grass in a pasture.

Every afternoon, in spring and summer and fall, Jay went to the pasture to drive the cows home.

On this afternoon, late in summer, he set out before sundown, eating a slice of buttered bread.

He walked along the lane on the side of a hill. The dust under his feet felt soft and warm. He spread his toes and watched the dust squirt between them.

After he had walked forward for a while, he turned around and walked backward for a while. As he walked, he looked at his footprints in the dust.

A hickory tree grew beside the lane. Its branches shaded the hillside. Nuts grew among its leaves.

With a stick Jay knocked a nut from a low branch.

He picked up the nut and smelled the tight green hull that enclosed it. The smell tingled in his nose like the smell of the first frost.

Jay put the nut in his pocket.

A creek flowed across the lane at the foot of the hill.

Jay waded into the creek.

The clear water rippling against his ankles cooled his feet. It washed them clean of dust.

Jay wiggled his toes in the smooth brown gravel on the bottom of the creek.

He picked up a small flat rock lying in the water. He turned it over. There was the print of a fern.

Jay put the rock in his pocket.

When Jay waded out of the creek he stood for a minute on the bank.

He watched a crayfish scuttling backward among the rocks.

He watched minnows darting about in the water.

At his feet he saw a gray goose feather. He picked it up, smoothed it with his fingers, and put it in his pocket.

A rail fence zigzagged between the creek and a cornfield.

As Jay walked toward the fence he heard a scratchy noise. He saw a gray lizard slithering along the middle rail.

He stopped. He stood very still and watched.

The lizard slithered away, out of sight.

Jay climbed the fence. He sat on the top rail.

He heard the wind rustling in the ripening corn.

He heard bugs and beetles ticking.

He heard a cicada fiddling high notes in the summer heat.

He heard an owl hooting in the woods.

Jay climbed down from the fence and walked between two rows of corn.

In the dirt he saw an Indian arrowhead, turned up by a plow. He picked it up, brushed the dirt from it, and put it in his pocket.

Beans had been planted with the corn. The vines climbed the tall cornstalks.

Jay picked a bean pod. With his thumb nail he opened it.

He shelled the beans into his hand. They were white, striped with red speckles. The stripes on every bean were different from the stripes on every other bean.

In Jay's hand the beans felt cool—like morning.

Jay put the beans in his pocket.

Jay climbed the steep pasture hill where an old apple tree stood. The russet apples that grew on one side of the tree were sweet. The red apples that grew on the other side of the tree were sour.

Jay picked a russet apple with one hand, and a red apple with the other. He took a bite from one apple, then a bite from the other—sweet and sour, sweet and sour.

As he ate, he looked off into the hollow below him. It was long and narrow. A road ran the length of it. At the end of the road stood a white schoolhouse.

Jay looked a long time at the schoolhouse. Then he turned and walked slowly down the hill toward the cows.

The cows looked up from their grazing. They switched their tails and started home. Nodding their heads and switching their tails, they walked, one behind another, along the cow path beside the fence.

Jay walked behind them.

Beside the cow path a cricket jumped.

Jay watched the cricket crawl underneath a stone.

Quietly he lifted an edge of the stone.

Quickly he cupped his hand over the cricket.

He gathered the cricket in both hands. Carrying it gently, he hurried after the cows.

Across the creek he waded.

Along the lane he trudged in the dust.

Into the barn he drove the cows. His father was waiting to milk them.

"What took you so long?" asked Jay's father.

"Nothing," said Jay.

Jay hurried to the house.

"What's that in your hands?" asked Jay's mother.

"Cricket," said Jay.

"What are you going to do with him?" asked Jay's mother.

"Keep him," said Jay.

"What will you do with him when you go to school?" asked Jay's mother.

"How many days till I go to school?" asked Jay.

"Five," said Jay's mother. "Next Monday you'll begin."

"Cricket will stay in my room and wait for me," said Jay.

"You'll need a cage to keep him in," said Jay's mother.

She opened a kitchen drawer and took from it a tea strainer. She tucked the handle of the strainer into Jay's pocket.

Off Jay hurried to his room.

He laid the strainer upside down on his table and put Cricket inside.

He brought Cricket water in a bottle cap.

He brought Cricket a piece of lettuce leaf, a thin slice of cucumber, and a slice of banana.

Cricket sat inside the tea strainer. Jay sat on his bed beside the table and watched.

Cricket sat and Jay sat.

Cricket did not drink the water.

He did not eat the lettuce, nor the cucumber, nor the banana.

"Jay, come to supper!" called Jay's mother.

Jay, on his bed beside the table, watched Cricket.

"Jay!"

After supper Jay hurried back to Cricket.

Some of the lettuce leaf was gone, Jay thought.

A nibble had been nibbled off the cucumber, he thought.

He sat on his bed beside the table and looked at Cricket.

"Do you like your new home, Cricket?" he asked.

Cricket sat and Jay sat.

The light in the room grew dim.

Night came.

Jay pulled the table closer to his bed. He got into bed and fell asleep.

A noise waked him. "Chee! Chee!"

Cricket was fiddling. Cricket was fiddling loud and clear. "Chee! Chee! Chee!"

Jay sat up in bed and listened.

"You do like your new home, don't you, Cricket?" he asked.

"Chee! Chee! Chee!" fiddled Cricket.

Jay reached under his pillow and found his flashlight.

He turned the flashlight on. The fiddling stopped.

Jay turned the flashlight off and put it under his pillow.

He lay down again. In the dark he waited, listening . . . listening.

"Chee! Chee! Chee!" fiddled Cricket.

The next day Jay made Cricket a cage out of a piece of wire screen. It was bigger than the tea strainer.

Every morning Jay brought Cricket fresh pieces of lettuce and cucumber and banana. He put fresh water in the bottle cap.

Every afternoon Jay shut the door of his room, turned Cricket out of his cage, and played with him.

Cricket jumped about the room. Jay jumped after him.

Cricket crawled up the curtain at Jay's window. He jumped to the door of Jay's closet.

"Don't let Cricket in that closet," said Jay's mother. "He might eat your new sweater. Then what would you wear to school?"

Every night, when Jay got into bed and the dark room grew still, Cricket fiddled.

"Chee! Chee! Chee!" And "Chee! Chee! Chee!"

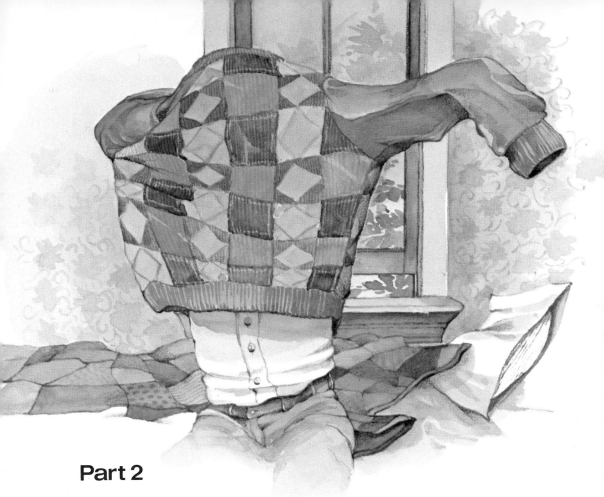

Part 2

Monday came.

Jay was ready for school early.

He said good-bye to Cricket. He looked at Cricket a long time.

"You'd better be going now," said Jay's mother. "You mustn't be late for the bus."

Jay said good-bye to his mother. He said good-bye again to Cricket. He started down the road.

When he had gone a few steps he turned and hurried back. He went into his room. He stood looking at Cricket.

"Jay!" called his mother.

Quickly Jay emptied his pocket. He piled on the table an Indian arrowhead, hickory nuts, buckeyes, and beans.

"Jay!"

Into his pocket Jay tucked Cricket. Away he ran down the road.

At the mailbox Jay waited.

Along came the yellow school bus. It stopped, and the driver opened the door. Jay climbed in. He sat down beside a window in the front of the bus.

The bus was filled with boys and girls. They talked and laughed.

"Chee! Chee!"

Inside Jay's dark pocket Cricket began fiddling.

The talking stopped. Everybody listened.

"Chee! Chee! Chee!" fiddled Cricket.

Jay cupped his hand against his pocket to quiet Cricket.

"Maybe somebody's taking a cricket to Teacher," said one boy.

Everybody on the bus laughed—everybody but Jay. He cupped his hand harder against his pocket.

"Chee! Chee! Chee!" fiddled Cricket.

"Maybe Towhead down there in front has that cricket," said another boy in the back of the bus.

Everybody on the bus looked at Jay.

Jay crowded against the window. He pressed his hand hard against his pocket. He looked straight ahead.

"Chee! Chee! Chee!" fiddled Cricket.

"I'd like to see Teacher when that cricket starts singing in school," said someone else.

Everybody on the bus laughed very loud— everybody but Jay.

WNSHIP PUBLIC SCHOOLS ★

When the bus reached the schoolhouse it stopped.

Jay waited until all the other boys and girls had got off. Then, pressing his hand against his pocket, he too climbed off.

He stood wondering where to go.

The driver smiled at him. "You belong in that room just inside the front door," he said to Jay. "Good luck with your cricket!" he added.

Jay looked at the other boys and girls in the schoolyard. They were calling to one another. They were laughing and talking.

Jay kept close to the fence as he made his way around them.

He found his room.

He found Teacher inside the room.

He told her his name.

He sat at the desk she pointed out to him.

Jay kept his hand pressed over his pocket. He sat still and waited.

A bell rang.

Teacher began talking to the children. The children listened. The room was very quiet.

"Chee!" fiddled Cricket.

Jay pressed his hand against his pocket to quiet Cricket.

"Chee! Chee! Chee!" fiddled Cricket.

The children turned in their seats. They giggled.

Teacher stopped talking. She looked about the room.

"Does someone have a cricket in this room?" she asked.

No one answered.

Teacher began talking again.

"Chee! Chee!" fiddled Cricket.

Teacher left the front of the room. She walked up and down between the rows of desks. As she walked, she talked to the children. As she talked, she listened.

She reached Jay's desk.

"Chee! Chee!" fiddled Cricket.

"Jay," Teacher asked, "do you have that cricket?"

Jay swallowed hard. He nodded his head.

"You'd better put it outside," said Teacher. "It's disturbing the class."

Jay sat very still. He looked at his desk. He pressed his hand hard against his pocket. He felt Cricket squirming.

"Jay," said Teacher, "put the cricket outside."

Still Jay sat. Still he looked at his desk.

"Jay," said Teacher, "aren't you going to put the cricket outside?"

Jay shook his head.

"Why not?" asked Teacher.

"I couldn't find him again," said Jay.

"Put him outside anyway," said Teacher. She waited.

Jay swallowed hard. He glanced up at Teacher. Then he looked at his desk again.

"You could find another cricket, couldn't you?" asked Teacher.

Jay shook his head. "It wouldn't be this one," he said.

"Chee! Chee!" fiddled Cricket.

Jay looked up at Teacher.

"Jay," said Teacher, "is this cricket your friend?"

Jay nodded his head.

"I see," said Teacher.

Teacher walked slowly to the front of the room.

"Boys and girls," she said, "this morning Jay has brought a cricket to class. It is something special. It is his friend. Jay, will you come to the front of the room and show the boys and girls your cricket? You can put him under this glass," she said.

She turned a water glass upside down on her desk.

Jay walked to the front of the room.

He took Cricket from his pocket.

He put Cricket under the upside-down glass.

"Tell the class about your cricket, Jay," said Teacher. "How did you catch him?"

Jay told the class how he had caught Cricket in the cow pasture.

The boys and girls asked Jay many questions.

"How long have you had Cricket?"

"What does he eat?"

"Where does he sleep?"

"How high can he jump?"

"Can he do tricks?"

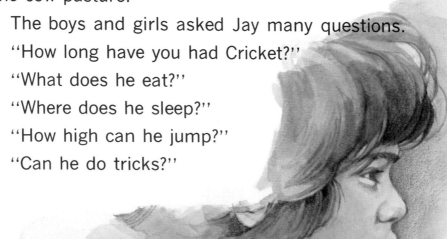

Jay answered all their questions.

"What makes him sing?" asked one girl.

"He doesn't sing," said Jay. "He fiddles with his wings."

"Tell him to fiddle now," said all the boys and girls.

"He likes to fiddle in the dark," explained Jay. "That's why he was fiddling in my pocket. It's dark in there."

"Does Cricket fiddle especially for you sometimes?" asked Teacher.

"Every night," said Jay.

"You may put Cricket back in your pocket now, Jay," said Teacher. "If he fiddles, he won't disturb us."

"What are you going to bring next, Jay?" asked a boy.

Jay thought of the stone with the print of a fern on one side. He thought of the gray goose feather. He thought of the Indian arrowhead.

He thought of the hickory nut, and of the smell of it that tingled in his nose like the smell of the first frost.

He thought of the beans.

He thought of the cicada fiddling high notes in the summer heat.

He thought of the russet apples and the red apples growing on the same tree—sweet and sour, sweet and sour.

He thought again of the beans—white, striped with red speckles, and, in his hand, cool, like morning.

"Beans," he said.

Rebecca Caudill

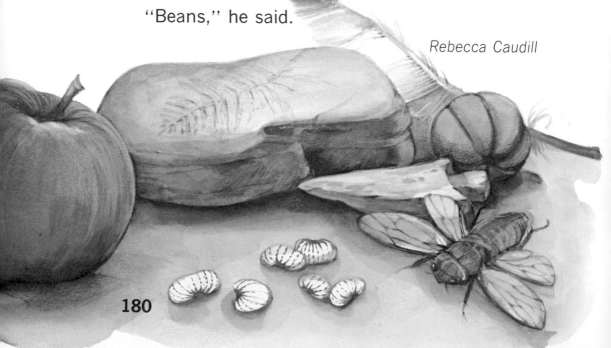

180

A Most Unusual Pet

Suppose you could have any pet you wanted—whether there really was such an animal or not. Would it be a giraffe with a red saddle like Maria's, a Snortsnoot, or a Blooplebee? What would it eat? Where would it sleep? Where would it play?

Think of a very unusual pet. When you have a pet in mind, describe it to your classmates. Your pet could be as unusual as a pink hippopotamus who eats only chocolate candy bars, likes to sleep in the bathtub, and runs through the flowers in the park.

On another sheet fill in the blanks for the pet you are thinking of.

I would like to have a _____ who would eat only _____. It would like to _____ and then _____. I would name my pet _____ and would keep it in _____.

Now that you have told about your unusual pet, try to make up a story about something that happened to the two of you one day.

Speaking of Dinosaurs

Discovering Dinosaurs

When you tell somebody that something happened a long time ago, you may mean that it happened a few years ago or before you were born or even before your father was born. But when you read that dinosaurs lived a long time ago it means that they lived a long, long, LONG time ago. That means long before your father was born and even long before your grandfather was born or your great great grandfather. Long before there were any towns. Before there were books. Before there were people. Before there was anything that you can see from your window now—except clouds and sky. And that *is* a very long time.

Dinosaurs lived on the earth millions and millions of years before there were any people. Nobody ever went dinosaur hunting because there wasn't any person living on the earth to go. So of course nobody ever met a live dinosaur in the woods or anywhere else.

Dinosaurs lived on the earth for a LONG, LONG, LONG time. They lived on many parts of the earth. Many of them lived on the part of the earth that is now the United States—in Wyoming, Colorado, Utah, Arizona, Texas, Montana, and in many, many other states. Of course, there was no United States then.

Dinosaurs ruled the animal world when they lived, millions of years ago. Some of them were the biggest of all animals. They were the fiercest animals. And there were more dinosaurs than any other kind of four-footed animals.

In those days there were no horses, no cows, no sheep, no squirrels. There were no birds. There were frogs and toads, but they were not like the ones we have today. There were fish in the sea, but they were not like our bass and trout. There were big sea turtles. Even though there were other animals on land and in the sea, those days of long ago were the days of the dinosaurs.

187

Even the trees and other plants did not look then as they do now. There were trees and bushes that looked like palms and evergreens, but there were no oaks and maples. There were no garden flowers and no vegetables. The animals and plants were very different then from the animals and plants that you see when you walk in the woods and fields. Dinosaurs lived in a very different world from ours.

What did a dinosaur look like? That's like asking, "What does a bird look like?" It depends upon what kind of a bird you are asking about. There are many kinds of birds. There are owls and bluebirds and ostriches. But bluebirds don't look like owls and owls don't look like ostriches. But bluebirds, owls and ostriches are all birds. There were many kinds of dinosaurs too. And they didn't look alike any more than birds do. There were thousands of kinds of dinosaurs.

Dinosaurs were all sizes and shapes. Some were terrible giant animals that were big enough to look over a house and see what was in the back yard. But of course there were no houses and no back yards in the days of the dinosaurs. Some of them were the biggest land animals that have ever lived on the earth. Some were as small as a cat that can scramble under your back yard fence. And some were middle-sized, like sheep or pigs. Some were a little larger, about the size of horses and cows. Some were still a little larger, about the size of elephants. Many of them were bigger than you can believe.

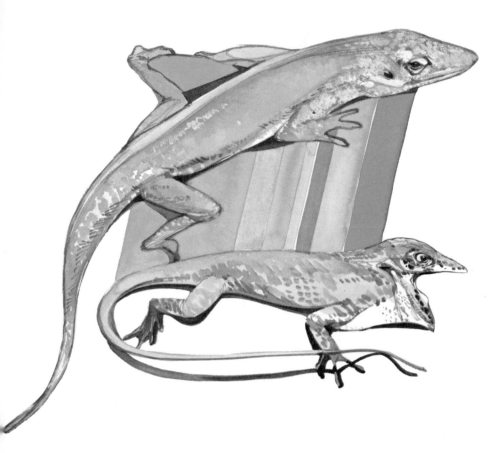

All dinosaurs were reptiles.[1] There are reptiles
living on the earth today, but they do not look
at all like the dinosaurs did. Snakes and lizards
and turtles are all reptiles. Crocodiles and
alligators are reptiles too. They all have scales
or hard parts on the outside of their bodies, and
they breathe with lungs.

1 reptiles (REP-tilz)

Dinosaurs spent much of their time roaming over the land looking for something to eat. Some ate smaller animals. Some of the large dinosaurs ate smaller dinosaurs, and some of the large ones killed and ate each other. Some ate plants of all kinds, and others were both plant eaters and animal eaters, and still others were only meat eaters.

The big ones lumbered along as they looked for animals and plants to eat. The little ones could run fast, and probably did. They chased other animals or went from one place to another to find new plants to eat.

Some dinosaurs spent much of their time in swamps or in the water. They found food there because the animals and plants they liked to eat lived there. Some kinds of dinosaurs got away from their enemies by hurrying into the water when enemies were after them.

Many of the dinosaurs walked on two strong hind legs. Their hind legs were longer than their front legs. Their hind legs were good for walking and their front legs for grabbing and holding food. There were long strong claws on their hind legs and on their front legs too. These claws were used to catch and hold and tear their food.

Many of the dinosaurs had strong teeth. Some had teeth for meat eating but more of them had plant-eating teeth. Can you tell what an animal eats by looking at its teeth? Look at your dog's teeth and you will see that he has sharp teeth for biting and tearing meat. Some of his teeth help him to hold on to his food. Some of them help to grind meat and get it ready for him to swallow.

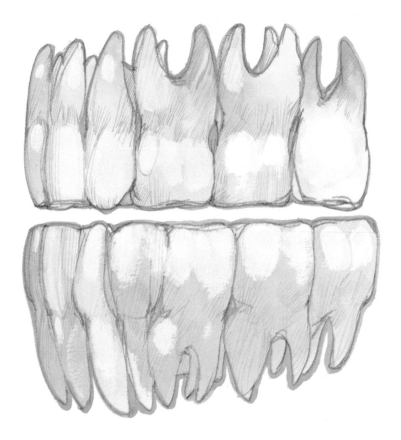

Your own teeth are good for eating both plants and meat. The front ones are for biting. The back ones are for chewing. Feel them with your tongue and you can tell how they are different from each other.

There were many exciting kinds of dinosaurs. The next story tells you about a few of the largest ones.

Glenn O. Blough

Dinosaur Differences

One of the first dinosaurs was very big. His body was as big as a truck or a small airplane. He had a long neck, a long tail and a very long name. His name was Brontosaurus.[1]

Brontosaurus liked the water. He stayed in the water as much as he could because it was easy for him to walk in the water. But it was hard for him to walk on land because he was so heavy.

[1] Brontosaurus (brahn-tə-SAWR-uhss); also called Apatosaurus (ə-pa-toh-SAWR-uhss)

198

Brontosaurus found much of his food in the water. And he needed a lot of food because he was so big. Brontosaurus was safe in the water. But he was not safe on land because there was another dinosaur on land that wanted to eat him. This dinosaur was called Allosaurus.[1]

When Allosaurus came near, Brontosaurus ran away. He ran through the mud. He splashed through the water. Allosaurus could not swim so he could not follow Brontosaurus into the deep water. When Brontosaurus got to the deep water, he was safe.

[1] Allosaurus (al-ə-SAWR-uhss); also called Antrodemus (an-trə-DEEM-uhss)

But some of the first dinosaurs did not live near water. One of these was Stegosaurus.[1] He lived on dry land and ate the plants there. Stegosaurus was one of the first dinosaurs to have armor. He had his armor on his back. The armor went all the way from his head to his tail and helped to keep Stegosaurus safe. Stegosaurus had a tail that kept him safe, too. On the end of his tail there were four long spikes. No other dinosaur wanted to get near those spikes. Not even Allosaurus. So if he was not very, VERY hungry, Allosaurus left Stegosaurus alone.

[1] Stegosaurus (steg-ə-SAWR-uhss)

Not all the dinosaurs lived at the same time. Scientists say that Brontosaurus, Allosaurus, Stegosaurus and many other dinosaurs lived for millions and millions of years. Then, one by one, they died out. Brontosaurus died out. Allosaurus died out. Stegosaurus died out, too.

But many new dinosaurs came to take their place. One of these new dinosaurs lived in the water, or near the water. His name was Trachodon.[1] Trachodon was a big dinosaur. He was as tall as a tall tree. He ate only plants and leaves. Trachodon had a long, wide tail that helped him to swim very well.

1 Trachodon (TRAK-ə-don)

Some of the new dinosaurs had horns. One kind of dinosaur had three horns. He had a little horn on the end of his nose, and he had two big horns above his eyes. His name was Triceratops.[1] Triceratops was a big animal, much bigger than a horse or a cow. He had small teeth. He ate only plants and leaves. But because of his horns, Triceratops was not afraid of any other animal. He was not even afraid of the most terrible dinosaur of all—Tyrannosaurus.[2]

[1] Triceratops (trigh-SEHR-ə-tops)
[2] Tyrannosaurus (ti-ran-ə-SAWR-uhss)

Tyrannosaurus was one of the last of the dinosaurs. He ate only other animals. He stood 20 feet tall. He could look over the top of a tall tree. From his nose to his tail he was almost 50 feet long. He was as long as a big truck. His teeth were as long as a person's hand. And his mouth was full of teeth. He was probably the most terrible animal that ever lived on the land.

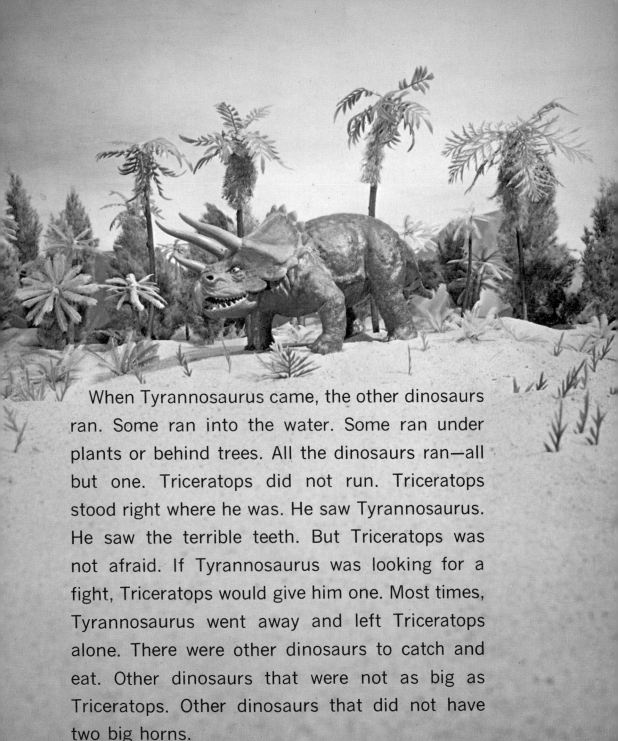

When Tyrannosaurus came, the other dinosaurs ran. Some ran into the water. Some ran under plants or behind trees. All the dinosaurs ran—all but one. Triceratops did not run. Triceratops stood right where he was. He saw Tyrannosaurus. He saw the terrible teeth. But Triceratops was not afraid. If Tyrannosaurus was looking for a fight, Triceratops would give him one. Most times, Tyrannosaurus went away and left Triceratops alone. There were other dinosaurs to catch and eat. Other dinosaurs that were not as big as Triceratops. Other dinosaurs that did not have two big horns.

But if Tyrannosaurus was very, VERY hungry, he stayed to fight. And what a terrible fight that must have been. The most terrible fight two animals ever had. Many times Tyrannosaurus won. Many times he was too strong for Triceratops, but not always. There were many times when Triceratops won, too. Triceratops must have been a brave animal. Any animal that stayed to fight with Tyrannosaurus must have been brave.

Then after millions and millions of years, something happened to the dinosaurs. All at once, they began to die out again. But this time no new dinosaurs came to take their place. Trachodon died out. Brave Triceratops died out. Even Tyrannosaurus, the most terrible animal that ever lived, died out too. At last there was not one dinosaur left in the world.

No one knows why all the dinosaurs died out. All we can do is guess what may have happened.

William Wise

Whatever Happened to All Those Dinosaurs?

This is a question that is easy to answer. They all died. There's not one left on the earth. They have been dead for millions of years. But when you ask "*Why* did they all die?" you are asking a very hard question. It is such a hard question that the best scientists in the world are not sure of the answer. They have ideas that may explain why these large, fierce dinosaurs all died. But no one is sure.

The first thing to remember is that the climate on the earth has not always been the same. It has changed from warm to cold and wet to dry and in other ways too. Once part of the United States and all of Canada were covered with a layer of ice many feet thick. Once many parts of the United States were covered with water. The earth has changed many times since animals and plants first lived on it.

Many scientists think that these changes in the climate may have caused dinosaurs to die. When the climate changed, many of the plants could no longer live. When the plants were gone the dinosaurs' food was gone. Even the dinosaurs who ate animals could not live if many of the plants died. This was because many of the animals they ate for food lived on plants. Scientists believe that changes in climate may be one of the reasons that dinosaurs died.

But many scientists think there were other reasons why dinosaurs died. Perhaps something happened to their eggs. Maybe some other animals found their eggs and ate so many that there were no more young dinosaurs. Or perhaps the change in climate kept the eggs from hatching. Some scientists believe that some dinosaurs may have eaten the eggs of other dinosaurs. But why would this happen all of a sudden? This is a puzzle that scientists have not solved.

Animals must be able to survive in the place where they live. Most water animals must be able to move about in the water. Water animals usually have fins or flippers or something else to push themselves through the water. They need gills to breathe under the water. Water animals cannot live on land.

If animals live on land they need legs or something else to move with. They need lungs for breathing. They must be able to protect themselves against their enemies. Land animals cannot live in water.

If the place where animals live changes, then the animals must change too. This takes a long, long time. Animals that live in water cannot suddenly live on land. Perhaps the dinosaurs were not able to change fast enough to keep up with the changes that took place on the earth. Perhaps that is why they all died. So when the swamps and seas and ponds dried up, the dinosaurs died.

Even though many dinosaurs were very large, many of them had very small heads and almost all of them had very small brains for such large animals. Some scientists think that this may have been one reason that they all died. Their brains were not very good, so perhaps they could not get away from their enemies or protect themselves in other ways. Maybe they just didn't have the brains to stay alive.

Glenn O. Blough

How Do We Know About Dinosaurs?

Finding Clues

If the dinosaurs died millions of years ago, and no one was alive to see them, then how do we know so much about them? How do we know what they looked like?

We know about dinosaurs from their bones. We have found many dinosaur bones. We have even found their eggs and their footprints. Does this seem hard to believe? Perhaps. The scientists themselves were surprised when the first bones were discovered.

But over the years the scientists learned much about the story of the dinosaurs. They worked very slowly. Sometimes they spent years putting together the bones from just one dinosaur.

The story began in 1818. The United States was a very young country then. Not a single railroad had been built. People traveled by wagon, by boat, on horses, or on their own feet.

In 1818 some strange bones were dug up in the valley of the Connecticut River. No one knew what kind of animal they had come from.

A few years later, some strange teeth were found in the rocks of Sussex, England. The woman who found them took them to her husband, Dr. Gideon Mantell. He was both a doctor and a scientist.

Dr. Mantell had never seen anything like these big teeth. He showed them to other scientists. They said the teeth had probably come from a rhinoceros.[1] But who ever heard of a rhinoceros in England? The rhinoceros belonged in Africa and Asia.

[1] rhinoceros (righ-NOSS-ər-əss)

Dr. Mantell took some tools to the place where the teeth had been found. He dug very carefully and found a number of strange bones.

He studied the bones for a long time. Finally he decided they had come from a large reptile. The teeth looked like those of a living lizard, the iguana.[1]

Later another scientist gave this strange reptile a general name. He called it a dinosaur, meaning "terrible lizard."

Even before the first dinosaur bones were dug up, strange footprints had been discovered in solid rock. Nobody ever thought that animals had made them.

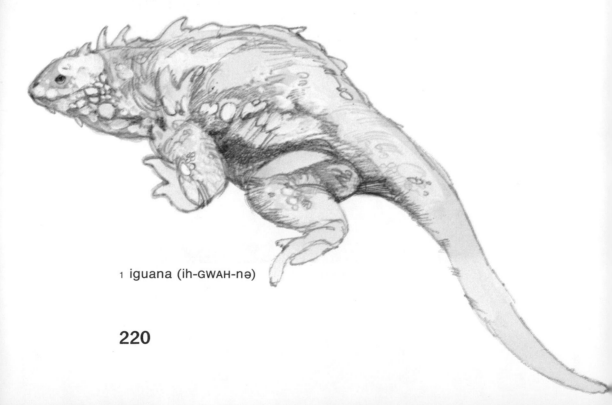

[1] iguana (ih-GWAH-nə)

The first footprints were reported in 1802. A Connecticut farmer was plowing his corn field. His plow struck a buried stone. He dug it out. It was marked with tracks like those of a large bird.

Other stones with tracks were found. Years later people learned that the tracks had not been left by birds. They had been made by dinosaurs that walked on their hind legs. These dinosaurs had three toes on each foot.

But how could the dinosaurs make tracks in hard stone? They couldn't. The tracks were made along the edge of a river or a shallow bay of the sea. Sometimes the water would spread over the shore, turning the hard ground into mud. Then the water would fall back.

The dinosaurs walked through the mud. Then the sun dried it and baked it. The footprints were as plain as a dog's tracks in a fresh concrete sidewalk.

When the water rose again, the footprints were filled with fine sand. After a great many years, the mud turned into hard rock. The giant tracks were still there. The water brought in more sand and mud, burying the tracks.

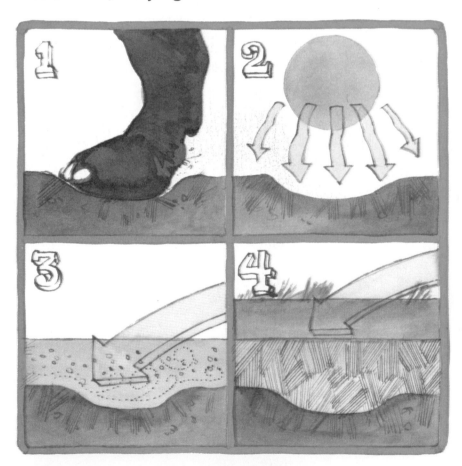

It was millions of years later that the Connecticut farmer plowed up the famous stone. There were the same tracks. They had been made by one of the thousands of dinosaurs that used to feed on plants in the river valley.

Dinosaur footprints have been found in many places besides Connecticut. Some of them are as long as the arm of a boy or girl.

Bones Become Fossils

Scientists have learned much about dinosaurs by studying their bones. These bones have been buried for millions of years and have turned to stone. They are called fossils.

In Arizona, a whole forest was turned to stone. It is called the Petrified Forest. There you can see hundreds of fossil trees lying on the ground. Some are whole. Others have broken into large chunks or small pieces. All of this wood was once buried. It became stone after thousands of years.

Some fossils show the print of leaves, ferns, and even insects. Long ago they lay in mud. After thousands of years the mud turned to stone.

These fossils tell us what the world was like millions of years ago. Fossils of palm trees and giant ferns have been found with the bones of dinosaurs. So we know they all lived at the same time.

Palm trees need warm weather. Giant ferns need plenty of rain. So there must have been more heat and rain than we have now.

At first, fossils were found only by mistake. They might be found on hillsides where roads were being built. Or when a basement was being dug. Or when a farmer plowed a field.

Usually fossils are not found on top of the ground. When scientists began to look for fossils, they hunted in deep valleys and canyons. They looked for places where the rocks had been washed bare by rain and running water.

The best place to look for fossils is desert country. The ground is not protected by trees and grass. Underneath there may be bones that have been buried for millions of years.

The desert gets much wind and some rain. In some places, the soil is blown away by the wind and carried away by the water. Then the bones underneath can be seen. This is where the work of the scientist who studies bones really begins.

Roy Chapman Andrews

Solving the Puzzle

Paleontologists[1] are scientists who know many things about rocks and how they were made. They are especially interested in the rocks that are made when mud and clay and sand settle out of water. These rocks are the ones most likely to have fossils in them.

1 paleontologists (pay-lee-on-TOL-ə-jəsts)

Paleontologists know a lot about where different kinds of rocks are found. When paleontologists go out on a scientific detective trip, they go where the right kinds of rocks are. Then they begin to look. They may find first a few small bones or teeth or other small fossils. They may find only tiny chips from bones, or they may find a part of a bone sticking out of the rock. Then they really begin to do some detective work. They may dig some of the rock away and find that the bone is not so small after all. It may turn out to be a very large bone. It may turn out to be many bones. It may be a whole group of bones that can be fit together and made into an animal frame. This bone frame is called a skeleton.[1]

1 skeleton (SKEL-ə-tən)

Digging these bones out of the ground or rock is not an easy job. Paleontologists can't do it as you would dig up a rock that you wanted to move out of your back yard. You would use a pick and shovel and other large tools. Paleontologists cannot do this because they may break the bones in the rocks. They often start by digging around the rock until they can see the outside of the bones. Then they dig under it very carefully and finally lift it out.

Paleontologists can't just dump the fossil rock into the back seat of their cars either. They must be sure that they won't break any of the bones, which may be as easy to break as an egg. When the bones are broken, they may be useless for study.

The fossil rock is usually covered with pieces of cloth and a paste that gets hard the way plaster for a wall gets hard. The paleontologist presses the cloth and paste into the rough places in the rock and covers it with cloth and plaster so that none of the bones will stick out and get broken. This cloth and hard paste protect the bones on their trip back to the laboratory. Often many large pieces of fossil rock are brought back from one scientific detective trip.

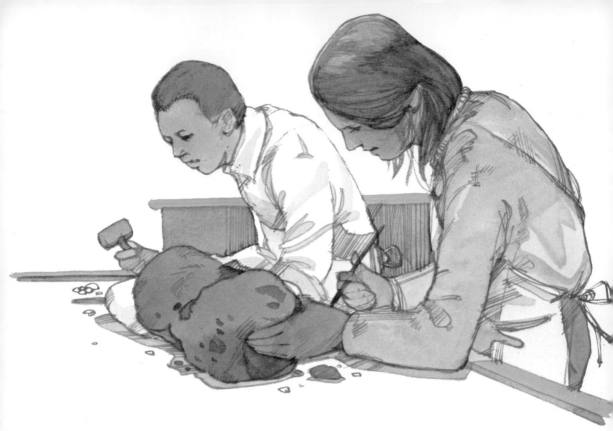

In the laboratory paleontologists begin to chip the rock away from the bones to see what they have really found. The work goes slowly and must be done very carefully with special tools. Finally the bones are separated from the rock and cleaned up.

Sometimes the bones fit together into a skeleton just as they come from the rock. But often they don't. Then the paleontologist must use everything known about animals and bones and fossils to help make a skeleton.

Paleontologists must know a lot about how bones fit together to make an animal skeleton. They study skeletons of all kinds of animals. They use whatever they know about bones and skeletons to fit together the bones that have been found. They fit the bones together the way you fit the parts of a puzzle together. Sometimes they find that the bones will not make a skeleton at all. But sometimes they discover that some of these bones will fit other bones found in another place and at another time. They may not be from the same animal but they may be from the same kind of animal.

Animal skeletons have been made from bones that have come from many different places. Scientists once worked more than fifty years to find the bones to make one skeleton in a museum. They collected the bones from dozens of different places.

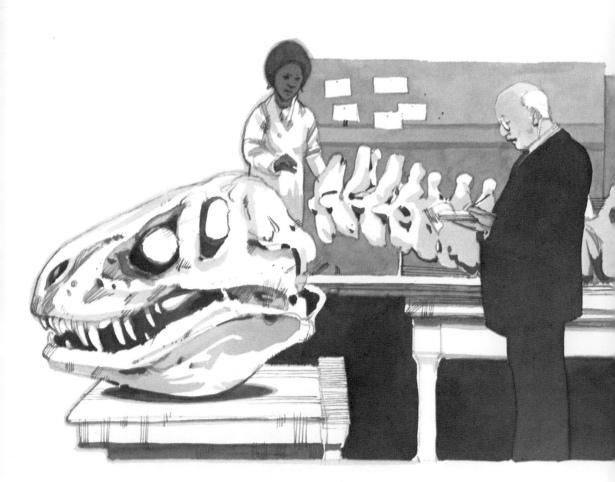

If you saved all the bones of a chicken and tried to put them together to make a skeleton, you would see that it is a very hard job. It is hard to tell how the bones fit together. It is even hard when you know what the skeleton of a chicken looks like. But suppose you had a pile of bones of an animal you had never seen. Then the job would be much harder. Remember that no one has ever seen a live dinosaur, and so scientists must work very carefully and do plenty of thinking about these bone puzzles. They must work the way you do when you are trying to put together a picture puzzle and you can't find the picture.

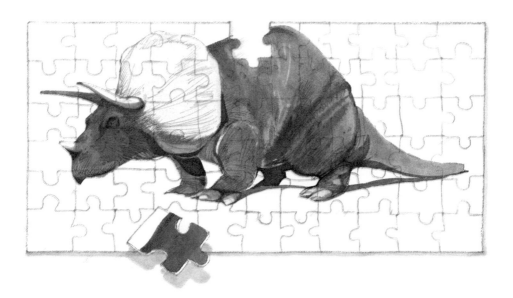

Paleontologists are like other scientists. They look carefully at things and they think about what they see. They sometimes must say, "I'm not sure about this. This may be the way these bones fit together. But it may not be." Years later someone may find the same kind of skeleton with all the bones in one place. Then the first scientist can be sure that the skeleton is put together correctly. But if the skeleton does not look like the new one, it must be changed.

Paleontologists do not rush through their work. They often say, "Wait a minute now. Let's be sure. Maybe this is true and maybe it is not. Let's get more facts." Scientists must work this way no matter what kind of puzzles they are trying to solve.

Glenn O. Blough

When Dinosaurs Were Roaming

A hundred million years ago
   In what is now Wyoming,
Midst Mesozoic jungle swamps
   The dinosaurs were roaming.

Some fed upon the leafy plants
   That grew along the shore,
While some ate those who ate the plants,
   Then looked around for more.

Some walked upon all fours, as you'd
   Expect of such a beast.
Some walked two-legged, like a man.
   There all resemblance ceased.

A few were small as dog or cat,
   But most were quite enormous.
Take BRONTOSAURUS, eighty feet
   In length, as books inform us.

So big was Brontosaurus that
  One brain would not suffice.
Besides the wee one in his head
  He had, and this was nice,

Another brain, or bunch of nerves,
  Placed rather near the rear
That doubtless had the duties of
  Assistant engineer.

And when an enemy drew near,
  This Brontosaurus slid
Into the water hurriedly,
  And there he wisely hid.

Who was this enemy he feared?
  Why was it that he fled him?
Well, it was ALLOSAURUS, and
  He had a right to dread him.

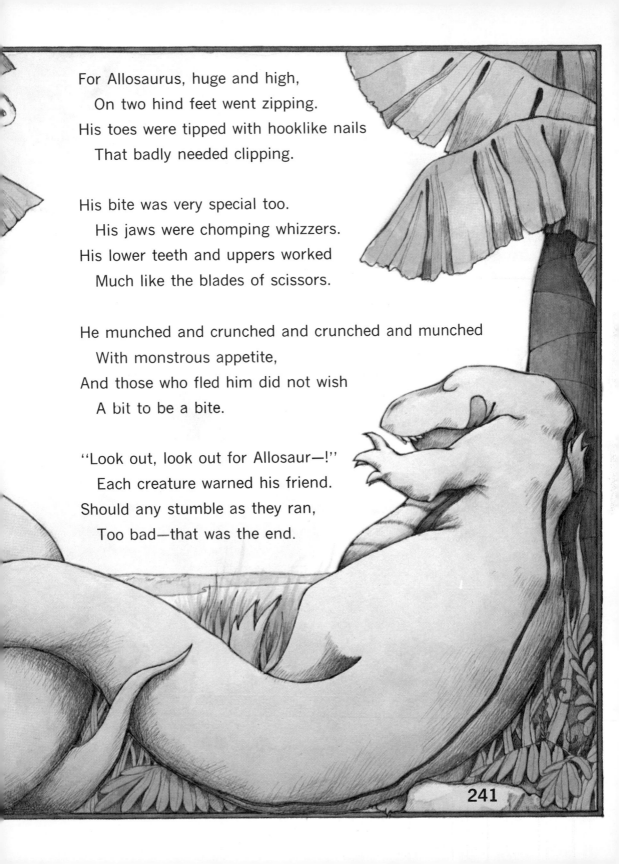

For Allosaurus, huge and high,
    On two hind feet went zipping.
His toes were tipped with hooklike nails
    That badly needed clipping.

His bite was very special too.
    His jaws were chomping whizzers.
His lower teeth and uppers worked
    Much like the blades of scissors.

He munched and crunched and crunched and munched
    With monstrous appetite,
And those who fled him did not wish
    A bit to be a bite.

"Look out, look out for Allosaur—!"
    Each creature warned his friend.
Should any stumble as they ran,
    Too bad—that was the end.

TRICERATOPS was well equipped
    With horns. His numbered three,
One on his nose's tip and two
    Where eyebrows ought to be.

And as for shields, to shield his neck
    From those who tried to grab it
He had a fancy bony frill
    He wore from force of habit.

What took the pleasure out of life
    For every living thing?
TYRANNOSAURUS REX. (The "rex"
    Means he was boss, or king.)

A tyrant was Tyrannosaurus,
    Forever seeking food.
The others, though they loved to chew,
    Weren't fond of being chewed.

242

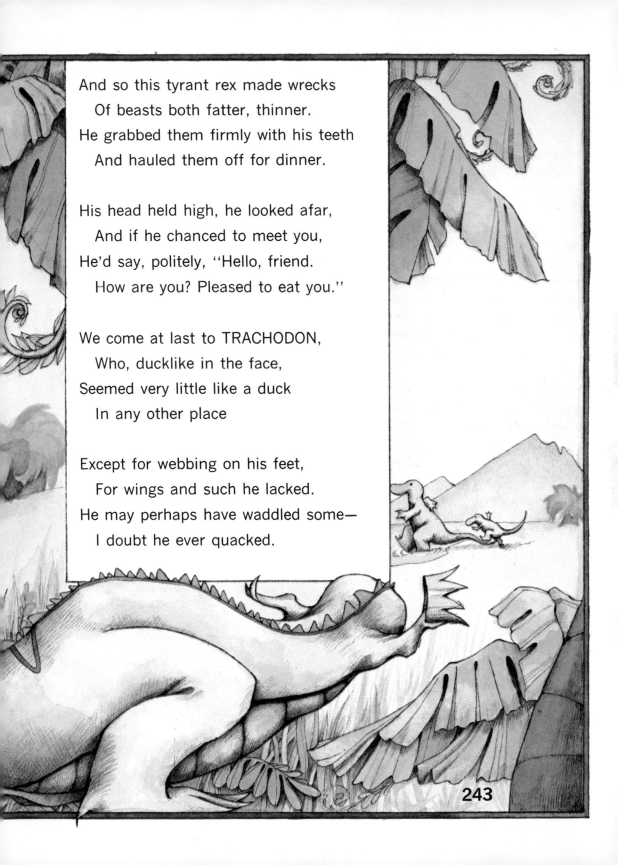

And so this tyrant rex made wrecks
 Of beasts both fatter, thinner.
He grabbed them firmly with his teeth
 And hauled them off for dinner.

His head held high, he looked afar,
 And if he chanced to meet you,
He'd say, politely, "Hello, friend.
 How are you? Pleased to eat you."

We come at last to TRACHODON,
 Who, ducklike in the face,
Seemed very little like a duck
 In any other place

Except for webbing on his feet,
 For wings and such he lacked.
He may perhaps have waddled some—
 I doubt he ever quacked.

243

This Trachodon stayed in or near
   The water all the time.
With ever-eager outstretched bill
   He slip-slopped through the slime.

He searched, you see, for tender slugs
   And cuttlefish and crabs,
All which he ate, along with plants,
   In gulps and dibs and dabs.

What made the dinosaurs die out
   Despite their strength and size?
Some blame it on their little brains
   And lack of enterprise.

Give thought, then, to the dinosaurs,
   Whom one no longer dreads.
They used their teeth and used their claws
   But didn't use their heads.

Richard Armour

Your-Own-O-Saurus

The names of dinosaurs are not just funny-sounding, strange words with no meaning. The different word-parts that make up the names of dinosaurs do have meaning. For example, *saurus* means *lizard. Dino* means *terrible.* So *dino·saurus* means *terrible lizard. Bronto·saurus* means *thunder lizard.*

Now that you know how the names of dinosaurs are made, read the sentences. Then, on another sheet, fill in what you think each dinosaur should be called.

This dinosaur has fifty legs and can run as fast as a horse. He is a _____ .

This dinosaur spends twelve hours a day eating. He will eat anything he can reach or catch. He is a _____ .

This dinosaur is very lazy and likes to spend most of the time sleeping. He is a _____ .

How would you describe a sneako·saurus? A grino·saurus? A singo·saurus?

Starlight and Sagebrush

247

SLUE-FOOT SUE
THE RAINMAKER

Pecos Bill was a very famous cowboy. So famous that other cowboys used to talk about him. "Pecos Bill," they said, "can throw a loop further than any cowboy. He can lasso a dozen cows safely in a single bundle. Pecos Bill is the greatest cowboy in the West."

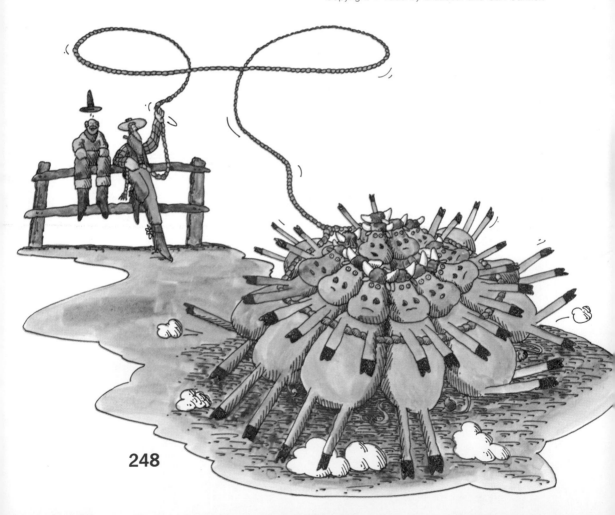

Pecos Bill broke many wild horses to the saddle. His favorite was a mustang called Widow-Maker. Other cowboys had tried to tame Widow-Maker but they failed. The horse had bucked and twisted so much that they were thrown off his back. Sometimes they were hurt badly. Only Pecos Bill could ride Widow-Maker.

Late one clear night, Bill rode Widow-Maker along the Pecos River. Thousands of stars were mirrored in the stream. Bill felt lonely. Then a round moon rose. It made the night as clear as day.

Bill saw a sight he would never forget. Down the shining river came a pretty girl riding bareback on a Texas catfish. The catfish was rearing and plunging and bucking. But the girl was riding him smoothly and easily. When she saw Bill, she edged the fish close to the river bank.

"My name is Slue-Foot Sue," she said. "I am the champion girl rider in all the west."

"You are very pretty too," said Bill.

"I like being a good rider better than being pretty," said Sue.

That afternoon Bill and Sue sat and talked. By
the end of the day they had decided to get married.

Folks came from miles around to the big
wedding party the next week. For wedding gifts
all the guests gave Bill and Sue lassos.

Slue-Foot Sue and Pecos Bill lived happily for a few months at their ranch beside the Pecos River. But no rains came in the spring. The yellow waters of the Pecos began to dry up. Not a drop of water fell from the sky. Sue had to keep her catfish in the old swimming hole. The rest of the river was too shallow for him to swim in. Widow-Maker galloped up the mountain every day. He drank the cold water from the melting snow near the top.

One night, all the Texas stars looked as if they had been cleaned and polished.

"Bill," Sue said to her husband. "Do we still have all those lassos we got for wedding presents?"

"They're in the woodshed," said Pecos Bill.

"Please get them," said Slue-Foot Sue. "I want you to tie them all together and make the longest lasso in the world. We are going to climb the mountain and I want you to bring the lasso along."

Bill looked puzzled.

253

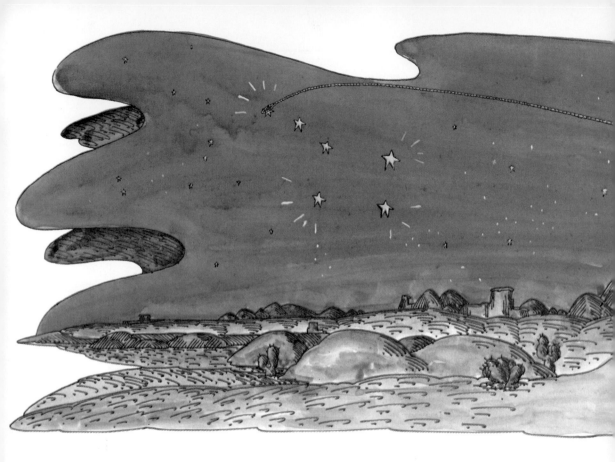

At the top of the mountain the stars looked even nearer and brighter than before.

Sue asked, "Do you see the Little Dipper?"

"Yes," said Bill.

"Can you throw our lasso over the handle?" asked Sue. "Then if we both pull hard enough we might tip the dipper. The water inside would pour out."

"A good idea," shouted Bill. "I can rope it. Just give me room to get the loop started!"

Soon the lasso was circling Bill's head. It made
a singing sound through the bright air. Bill kept
adding more rope to its length. At last, with one
great toss, Bill let it go. Up, up it went toward the
stars of the Little Dipper. Sue and Bill waited. It
seemed a long time before the line suddenly
tightened.

"I've got it," shouted Bill. "Now pull."

Pull they did, as hard as they could. Slowly the handle of the Little Dipper began to turn. Bill and Sue pulled even harder and the handle moved a little more. All night they tugged and tugged at the long rope.

Finally Sue said, "The Little Dipper's tipped enough. The water must be spilling. Let's tie the lasso fast and go home."

Daylight had begun to appear. Then suddenly there came a spatter of raindrops as big as oranges. Soon a steady stream of rain poured from the Dipper.

Bill and Sue walked home wet and happy. The falling rain washed the dusty brown trees and turned them green. The shining brown Pecos River overflowed its banks. Widow-Maker was drinking from it. Sue's catfish swam about joyfully.

Suddenly the rays of the rising sun struck the falling water. The biggest rainbow ever seen anywhere arched across the Texas sky.

Elizabeth and Carl Carmer

A Peanut

A peanut sat on the railroad track,
His heart was all a-flutter—
Choo-choo train comes 'round the bend,
Toot toot! Peanut butter!

I Scream, You Scream

I scream,
You scream,
We all scream
for ICE CREAM.

I Eat My Peas With Honey

I eat my peas with honey,
I've done so all my life,
It makes the peas taste funny,
But it keeps them on my knife!

Fuzzy Wuzzy

Fuzzy Wuzzy was a bear,
Fuzzy Wuzzy had no hair,
Then Fuzzy Wuzzy wasn't fuzzy,
Was he?

The Dancing Stars

An Iroquois Legend

Once upon a time, when the earth and sky were new, there lived seven little brothers. They loved to play and dance in the forest, and no matter where they went, they always went there together.

One evening as they were returning from the forest, they heard from far, far away the sound of someone singing. The song was not like any song they had ever heard before. It was so beautiful and mysterious the seven brothers completely forgot about going home. Instead they danced off in the direction of the song.

As the little boys danced, their feet seemed to grow lighter. Suddenly night came. Then, before long, they could see the forest and the houses of their people stretched out far below them in the moonlight. They saw that they were dancing right up in the sky. Higher and higher they danced, and the song grew louder. Still higher they danced, and the song grew louder and sweeter still.

"I came," sang the sweet voice, "for a hunter chased me, and now I am lost in the sky. But sleep, my little ones, in your warm dark cave. I will watch over you here in the sky."

Then the brothers saw a great black bear. She had a long tail made of stars, and she wore a necklace and belt made of white and shining clamshells. Stars twinkled at her nose and her toes, and the clamshells, too, sparkled like bright stars. It was she who was singing the sweet song the boys had heard, and they danced closer to her.

The great bear's song was beautiful, and they danced a long time to it. But at last they wanted to go home, for it was very late, but they did not remember the way. They begged the moon to show them how to go back, but the moon only smiled and said:

"This is your home now, my children. We welcome you, I and the stars, for we enjoy watching you dance." And the boys went on dancing, and strangely enough, they found that they did not grow tired at all. The bear's song grew louder and sweeter. Behind each boy a bright star grew, and the moon smiled at their dance.

Then the smallest star boy heard a tiny voice from far away. Someone was crying and calling his name. Over the sound of the bear's song and of his brothers' dancing feet he listened, and he heard the distant voice again. It was his mother's voice. The smallest boy began to run as fast as he could go, with the bright star he was wearing making a shining trail behind him.

"Come back, come back," cried his brothers and the moon, but the little boy raced away from them. Down he flew, past the eagle's nest, past the clouds, and closer and closer to the earth, as the sound of his mother calling him grew louder and louder.

Soon he could see her. She could almost touch his hand. Then he landed on the earth. But where he landed there was no boy. There was only a hole, the kind a star makes when it falls. His mother cried still harder when she saw the fallen star. Then she looked up and saw her other boys dancing in the sky.

"Stay there. Stay there," she called to them over the great bear's song, for she did not want them to fall, too. They heard her, as they danced far away and high in the sky, and they nodded their heads to show her they would obey.

The mother wept for the fallen star, and where her warm tears fell, a little green shoot sprang up. Higher and higher the green shoot grew. It was the smallest brother reaching for the sky, so he could be with his brothers again. Higher and higher it grew, until it reached the place where the brothers danced and the great bear sang.

"Welcome, dear brother," said the dancing star boys to the tall pine tree who had come to join them.

The pine tree is still there, the tallest tree in the forest. And you can see the brothers dancing even now, in the night sky, while the great bear sings her little bears to sleep.

Retold by Anne Rockwell

The Cool Ride in the Sky

It was a very hot summer day.

All the animals were hiding from the sun under bushes or underground, but not the buzzard. He was sailing around in the sky looking for food.

He'd been sailing around for hours, when suddenly—

A rabbit hopped out of his house. The buzzard quickly spotted him and swooped down, but the rabbit hopped back in his house.

270

The buzzard landed beside the rabbit's house.

"Hello rabbit," said the buzzard sweetly. "How is it down in your house?"

"Hot!" cried the rabbit. "It's hot in my house and it's hot on the ground. How is it up in the sky?"

"Oh rabbit," said the buzzard. "It's as cool as can be. Why don't you jump on my wings and I'll take you up there?"

The rabbit peeked out of his house. The sun was blazing hot.

"Hurry rabbit," said the buzzard. "I don't have time to be giving free rides to everyone."

The rabbit looked at the buzzard. The buzzard looked so cool and pleased that the rabbit decided to take a chance.

"Okay," he said, and hopped onto the buzzard's wings.

The buzzard flew up in the sky. He sailed around and around, until he was ready for lunch. "Hold on rabbit," he said. "I'm going down for a landing."

Then the buzzard went into his power dive, a hundred feet straight down. Just before he hit the earth, he shot up again throwing the rabbit to the ground. The buzzard then turned in the air, flew back to the ground and ate the rabbit for lunch.

Late that afternoon the buzzard was hungry again. He flew to the same place and circled around in the sky, around and around, until—

A squirrel scampered down from his nest. Quickly the buzzard headed for the squirrel, but the squirrel dashed back into a hole in the tree.

The buzzard landed on one of the branches.

"Hello squirrel!" the buzzard called. "How are you feeling today?"

"I'm hot, buzzard. It's been hot all day and I'm still hot."

"It's cool in the sky, squirrel. Jump on my wings and I'll take you up there."

Now the squirrel *knew* the buzzard was a tricky animal, but he also knew that the higher in a tree you go, the cooler it is, still—

"Jump on my wings," said the buzzard, "or maybe you're afraid to fly so high?"

"Of course not!" said the squirrel. He jumped onto the buzzard's wings and up they flew.

Meanwhile, a monkey who was sitting in the branches of a nearby tree had been watching the buzzard. He'd seen the trick the buzzard had played on the rabbit, and now he was watching to see what the buzzard would do with the squirrel.

The buzzard sailed around and around.

After a while the buzzard turned to the squirrel and said: "Hold on, squirrel. I'm going down for a landing."

Again the buzzard went into his power dive, a hundred feet straight down, shooting up again at the last minute, throwing the poor squirrel to the ground. Then the buzzard turned, flew back and ate the squirrel for dinner.

After the buzzard had flown off, the monkey began to swing on his branch. Back and forth, back and forth until—he got an idea.

The next day it was hot again. The sun was shining brightly, and the animals were hiding from the sun. But the monkey was standing in plain sight watching the sky.

When the other animals saw the monkey standing hour after hour in the hot sun, they became more and more curious and poked their heads further out of their hiding places.

Towards noon, the monkey spotted the buzzard. He began to dance up and down, flapping his arms in the air. In less than a minute the buzzard was down on the ground beside the monkey.

"Hello monkey," he said. "What kind of dance were you doing?"

"A flying dance. Did you like it?"

"Well . . . yes—"

"Yes," said the monkey. "I was doing a flying dance, just *wishing* I could go for a cool ride in the sky."

"Oh-h monkey!" The buzzard's face broke into a great big grin. "There's nothing I like more than giving free rides in the sky. Quick, jump on my wings and up we go."

The monkey winked at the other animals and slowly seated himself on the buzzard's wings.

The buzzard took off. He circled around once in the sky. Then he turned to the monkey and said: "Hold on monkey, I'm going down for a landing."

"HOLD ON!" the monkey shouted back. "THERE'S GOING TO BE NO MONKEY DINNER TONIGHT!"

And the monkey whipped his tail out and wrapped it tight around the buzzard's neck.

"BUZZARD!" said the monkey, "YOU STRAIGHTEN UP AND FLY RIGHT!"

The buzzard was caught and had to fly straight on.

The monkey ordered the buzzard to fly low, so he could wave to his friends on the ground. They cheered and waved back.

"Now then buzzard," said the monkey, "up we go." And the buzzard flew up again in the cool air and sailed around in the sky, until—

The *monkey* was ready to go down. The monkey loosened his hold ever so slightly on the buzzard's neck, and the buzzard glided down to a soft landing.

All the animals crowded around the monkey laughing and cheering, while the buzzard flew off in shame.

"We won't be seeing that buzzard again for a long time," said the monkey.

Then he flapped his arms in the air and began to hop from foot to foot. He was doing the flying dance.

And soon all the animals joined him.

Told by Diane Wolkstein

281

Ladies and Jelly Spoons

Ladies and jelly spoons:
I come before you
To stand behind you
And tell you something
I know nothing about.

Next Thursday,
The day after Friday,
There'll be a ladies meeting
For men only.

Wear your best clothes
If you haven't any,
And if you can come
Please stay home.

Admission is free,
You can pay at the door.
We'll give you a seat
So you can sit on the floor.

282

BETTY BOTTER

Betty Botter bought some butter.
But she said, "This butter's bitter!
If I put it in my batter,
It will make my batter bitter.
If I bought some better butter,
It would make my batter better!"
So she bought a bit of butter
Better than her bitter butter,
And she put it in her batter,
And her batter wasn't bitter.
So 'twas better Betty Botter
Bought a bit of better butter.

Giant of the Timber

CHARACTERS

STORYTELLER	PAUL'S MOTHER
FIRST LOGGER	PAUL'S FATHER
SECOND LOGGER	PAUL BUNYAN
THIRD LOGGER	A NEIGHBOR
FOURTH LOGGER	BABE, the blue ox
FIFTH LOGGER	*(two people under*
SIXTH LOGGER	*a blanket)*

TIME

The nineteenth century.

PLACE

Different sections of the northern United States.

STORYTELLER

Paul Bunyan is one of our best known American folk heroes. Hundreds of stories have grown up around him. Some tell how he came down from Canada. Others say that he appeared first in the West. And still others, that he was born in New England and went west as a young man to clear land. Whether there really was a man of Paul's size doesn't matter. He was the spirit of the United States.

(The STORYTELLER *steps off and six children in jeans and wool shirts come in and sit down on the other side of the stage.*)

FIRST LOGGER

Sure, he was born in Minnesota. Didn't he clear land all across the state and start the biggest lumber business in the world?

SECOND LOGGER

Well, I heard how he came down from Canada. That's why he dug the St. Lawrence River. So many people got mixed up about which country was which that Paul thought a river would be a good way of telling them apart.

THIRD LOGGER

You're all wrong. He was born in Maine. My grandfather was there at the time and he told just why it was Paul left. It was like this . . . (*The* THIRD LOGGER *crosses the stage to the other side where he enters a scene with* PAUL'S MOTHER *and* FATHER.) Even when he was a little boy his father and mother knew he was no ordinary baby.

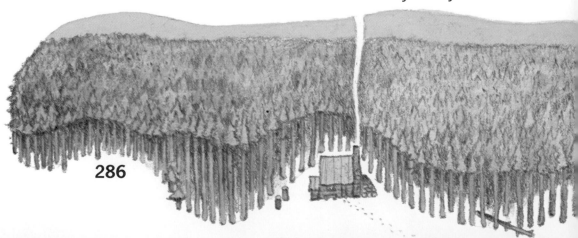

PAUL'S MOTHER

I think he's going to be president, Pa. He's grown faster and learned more in four months than any child I ever saw.

PAUL'S FATHER

He'll do big things, if he keeps on like this. Might be a sea captain or an explorer.

THIRD LOGGER

(*Now walking into the scene.*) How's the new baby, Mrs. Bunyan? I hear he's a big fellow.

PAUL'S MOTHER

(*Proudly.*) Land sakes, you haven't seen him yet! Eighty pounds when he was born, and growing like a weed.

PAUL'S FATHER

He's smart, too. All our children talked early but Paul, he's saying whole sentences already and he's only four months old.

THIRD LOGGER

Where is he? I'd like to see him.

PAUL'S MOTHER

Well, you'll have to come down to the beach. He got too big for me to handle, so his pa made a cradle for him out of a boat. We put him in it last week.

PAUL'S FATHER

It's in the bay where the waves can rock him all day long. Now all we have to do is carry his milk down to him.

THIRD LOGGER

But aren't you afraid he'll fall out?

PAUL'S FATHER

No, it's not very deep down there. And besides it's a flat-bottomed boat. You can see it from the door.

THIRD LOGGER

You mean that there's your baby? Why, he looks like a full grown man! Long black hair—and waving his arms around like that—

NEIGHBOR

(*Running in.*) Mr. Bunyan, Mr. Bunyan, come out quick! The baby, he—

PAUL'S FATHER

What's the matter?

PAUL'S MOTHER

What's happened? Did something happen to Paul?
(She starts off but stops when the NEIGHBOR
speaks.)

NEIGHBOR

No, *he's* all right. But he just rolled over in his
cradle, the way babies do, and it's causing a tidal
wave! You've got to move him before the whole
village is flooded out!

(All exit and the THIRD LOGGER *returns to his
circle.)*

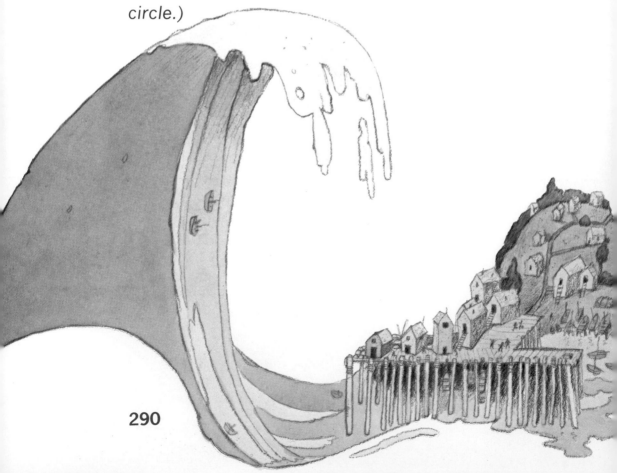

THIRD LOGGER

And that's the truth because my grandfather lived there and heard it. Well, after a few more scares like that, the state of Maine suggested politely that Paul go some place else.

FOURTH LOGGER

I can tell you where he went after that.

FIFTH LOGGER

He was smart enough but I heard they always had trouble with him in school because he was too big for the desks.

SIXTH LOGGER

Nothing was built for a child that size. So after a couple of years he quit school and just went on teaching himself.

FOURTH LOGGER

Well, next he was heard of was up in Canada. And that's why some folks say he came from those parts. It was the Winter of the Blue Snow and Paul was living by himself, trying to decide what to do with his life. He knew there was great work for him to do but up to then he wasn't sure just what it was.

(PAUL *walks out on the other side of the stage. He is the largest boy on stage.*)

PAUL

Blue snow! They wouldn't believe it back in Maine if I told 'em. And if I sent them some, by the time it got there, it would be melted. *(Stops, then speaks again.)* Just as cold as it is blue, too. *(He walks a few steps.)* Thought I heard something. Sounded like an animal. Not very old and maybe hurt. Likely freezing in this weather. *(He calls in a big voice.)* Where are you? Can you hear me? *(Pause.)* Over here, little fellow? *(He moves to the side of the stage and discovers a* BLUE OX. *It can be two people covered with a blue blanket and a paper bag mask on the head of the one in front.)* A little blue calf! Just a baby and out alone in all this weather. Seems to me you need food of some kind mighty quick. *(He pulls some bread out of his knapsack and offers it to the calf.)* That's the fellow. If you eat like that, you'll grow up into a big blue ox. *(Thoughtfully.)* You know, you're alone and I'm alone, little fellow. There's work in this world for both of us. Maybe, if we pull together, we'll discover what it is.

FOURTH LOGGER

And that's how Paul got Babe, the famous Blue Ox, that worked with him as long as he lived.

FIRST LOGGER

Everybody knows about the Blue Ox. Seemed like after that Paul knew that lumber was his business and Babe, he took to it like a duck to water. As fast as Paul chopped down the trees, Babe carried 'em off.

SIXTH LOGGER

And lots of other things happened too. Some of them good and some of them not so good.

FIRST LOGGER

But the thing about Paul was that he could turn a calamity into good luck. Like the time he made popcorn balls.

THIRD LOGGER

(Passing a bowl of popcorn.) Say, I almost forgot. How about some for old time's sake?

(All the loggers help themselves; then the SIXTH LOGGER goes on with his story.)

SIXTH LOGGER

Paul always liked popcorn. I remember how he used to sit thinking and eating popcorn at night by the fire. And the harder he thought, the faster he ate. Used to eat up a couple of baskets' full when he was thinking hard.

FIRST LOGGER

Well this time it all started with the popcorn blizzard. It was hot that summer and even the corn, which can take plenty of heat, was drying up on the stalks.

(The attention shifts to another part of the stage where PAUL *and the* FIRST LOGGER *are talking together and looking over a cornfield which is in the direction of the audience.)*

PAUL

Seems like even the corn is burning up this summer. Don't know what we'll feed the men if we lose this crop.

FIRST LOGGER

Look! Something's happening over there! The ears are beginning to burst!

PAUL

Where?

FIRST LOGGER

Over there! Watch out! It's exploding!

(The two duck as popcorn peppers the stage.)

PAUL

Looks like snow. If I wasn't so hot, I'd think it was a blizzard. I'm beginning to cool off just watching it.

FIRST LOGGER

The whole crop's popping. Do you suppose we can do anything with it?

PAUL

We'll see. That's an awful lot of corn to just let blow up. *(He picks up a kernel and tastes it thoughtfully.)* You know, it's not bad. *(Tastes another.)* Not bad at all. In fact, it's pretty good. Here, you eat some. Why not collect it in baskets and serve it up to the men?

297

FIRST LOGGER

(Tasting some.) It *is* good, only it's kind of hard to eat—one piece at a time. It would be easier if we could think of a way to hold a lot in our hands—

PAUL

I know! We can pour molasses over it so it sticks together. Ought to taste pretty good and it would be as easy to handle as bread.

FIRST LOGGER

(Returning to his group.) And that's what we did. From that day on there've been popcorn balls.

SECOND LOGGER

Sometimes I think Paul did more to change the ways of America than anyone else.

FOURTH LOGGER

And the map! Why, if I had time, I could tell you how he moved rivers and lakes!

FIFTH LOGGER

And dug Puget Sound!

SIXTH LOGGER

And made the Thousand Islands!

FIRST LOGGER

And started Old Faithful erupting!

SECOND LOGGER

And made the Pacific Ocean salty!

THIRD LOGGER

But we don't have time today. We'll have to save those stories for another night around the fire. But not one of us who knew him will ever forget them or the fact that Paul Bunyan was a giant.

STORYTELLER

Yes, Paul Bunyan *was* a giant. A big man who knew he was cut out for big things and he set out to do them.

(The STORYTELLER *goes off on one side and the group of* LOGGERS *go off on the other.)*

Nellie McCaslin

300

Bigger Than Life

Paul Bunyan and Slue-Foot Sue are characters from tall tales. Tall tale characters are often very big, bigger than any ordinary person. They can always do something better than anyone else.

If you were to tell a tall tale, who would be in it? Use the chart below to help you think of tall tale people. Maybe someone can hit more home runs than anyone else; you might call her Home Run Hazel. What do you think Menu Martin or Maxie Maps or Diamond Don does better than anyone else? What would be a name for a character who can run faster than anyone else? Or grow bigger apples?

What do I do better than anyone?	What is my name?
hit home runs	Home Run Hazel
?	Menu Martin
run faster	?
?	Maxie Maps
grow bigger apples	?
?	Diamond Don

Now try making up some of your own tall tale characters. Tell the group about them.

Amigo

By BYRD BAYLOR SCHWEITZER

Illustrated by GARTH WILLIAMS

His mother said,
"Come, Francisco, my son.
Tell me why your eyes are sad,
My little one."

His father said,
"How quiet you are.
Let me play you a tune
On my old guitar."

Plink.
Plink.
He strums the guitar,
Singing,
"Troubles run.
Fast and far . . .
Past the mountains
Behind a star."
Plink.
Plink.
A-plink.

Francisco listened to the song.
Then he told them what was wrong.

"You know, I want a dog. Any dog. A hound . . .
A dog I'll call Amigo and he'll follow me around
Wherever I go. Wherever I go
He'll be there.
Some days I'll follow him
Just to make it fair."

Francisco's mother turned with a sigh.
Francisco's father looked off at the sky.
"No, Francisco. It's all we can do
Just trying to feed your brothers and you."

307

Francisco seldom thought about
The things he had to do without
Because
He thought about the things he had.
In his mind he tried to add them up . . .
So many brothers.
So many jokes.
So many miles of desert all around.
So many cactuses. So many mountains—
So many places where caves can be found.
And
Plenty of wishes
To wish on a star.

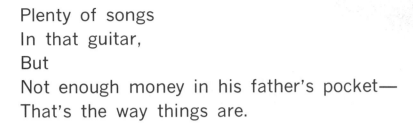

Plenty of songs
In that guitar,
But
Not enough money in his father's pocket—
That's the way things are.

Francisco's father mines for gold.
He knows he'll find it before he's old,
But
He hasn't found it yet
So he has to say,
"No, Francisco.
Another mouth to feed
Is one more than I need.
You just forget
About a pet."

His mother asked,
"What's small and wild
And can feed itself?
We'll have that, my child."

"But *what*?" Francisco frowned.

"You could tame a bird,
A bright wild bird
With the sweetest song
You ever heard."

"No. No. I can't fly.
He could go much
Higher than I."

"Up in the mountains
There are wildcats.
You can catch one if you're bold.
Here in the valley
There are tortoises one hundred years old."

"A tortoise is too slow for my fast feet,
And wildcats won't play in the desert heat."

"How about a lizard?
How about a quail?
How about a coyote
With a yellow tail?"

"No. No. And I don't want a frog."
Francisco shook his head,
He had to have a dog.

Suddenly his mother whirled around.
Her voice came out with a laughing sound.
"Ah, Francisco, my son!
A PRAIRIE DOG!
Could that be the one?"

They all laughed.
"A PRAIRIE DOG."
It seemed so funny—
He's more like a ground squirrel
Or a mouse or a bunny
Than a dog . . .
A strange little creature
With fast little feet,
Who doesn't mind
The desert heat.

"A prairie dog would be easy to find.
Of course, I had a *real* dog in mind
But
If I try
I think that I
Could love
A prairie dog . . .
A tiny black-eyed, run-around
Hole-in-the-ground
Squeak-a-dry-sound
Prairie dog,
A very
Merry
Prairie
Dog.''

Francisco's father said,
"You'd have to win his love
Before you tame him.''

"Yes, I will win his love.
Then I will name him
Amigo.
That's the name I was saving
For some big hound—
But I think it will do
For a little run-around.''

His mother smiled.
"How do you tame a prairie dog,
A thing that's wild?
How do you make him walk beside
A human child?"

"I'll give him presents
Like water and seeds
And tall sweet weeds.
I'll give him love
And whatever he needs."

Francisco hurried
To Prairie-Dog Town.
Very quietly
He sat down
On a rocky slope
To watch and wait
And dream and hope.

Prairie-Dog Town is a town under ground,
All tunnel and burrow and hilly mound . . .
The busiest town for miles around.
Ten little heads popped out of the earth
And looked around curiously
And jabbered furiously
And frowned at Francisco for all they were worth.

He wanted them to know that he
Was a friend, a brother,
Wanted them to see him
Simply as another
Desert creature
Who meant no harm.
So he lay down
With his head on his arm.
The sun was warm.
He nestled deep
Into clumps of grass.
Time passed. And then,
Francisco fell asleep.

When he opened his eyes
There wasn't a sound.
He sat up
And looked around
And found
One prairie dog still sitting in his place.
He seemed to be studying Francisco's face.

"Can that be Amigo?
Does he read my mind?
Does he know he's the one
That I came to find?"

Very gently he whispered
"Amigo . . ."
The word
Was so soft
It could only be heard
By one prairie dog
And one low-flying bird . . .
"Amigo . . ."
It was half laugh, half song,
The kind of word that floats along.

That day wherever Francisco went
He went with his dreams and he went content.
And he went with a hop and he went with a hope
And he jumped over rocks like an antelope.

Now you know Francisco
And the way he planned
To tame him a friend
In that desert land.
But you still don't know—
Though you very soon will—
What creature was hiding
Behind that hill . . .

Look
Toward the mountain,
There
Toward the sun.
See that brown speck
Dart and run?

That is Amigo.

The desert is wide
And the rocks are tall.
You might not notice
A creature so small.
But that is Amigo,
The prairie-dog child
Who runs with the wind
When the wind runs wild.

Just one summer old,
Adventurous and bold,
He's small enough to look
A tortoise in the eye,
Or exchange remarks
With a passing fly,
And brave enough to jump
At stars in the sky—
He never really caught one
But he likes to try.

Yes, this is Amigo . . .
Always full of ideas,
Saying summer is *his*—
And maybe it is—
To run through.

But should he be running
So fast and so far?
Why isn't he home
Where his brothers are,
In the dim burrows
Which wind far down
Below the surface
Of Prairie-Dog Town?

There
Old prairie dogs sit in the sun
Keeping watch through the summer day
While the little ones dodge in and out
Like children at play.

But Amigo isn't there.
He's *everywhere*,
Following every path he knows.
He doesn't worry,
He only *goes* . . .

And where is he going?
What does he seek?
Why does he gaze
At the mountain peak?

Amigo runs to a certain hill.
There he stops and waits until
He hears the sound of a boy's easy laughter.
Then he knows he's found what he came after:
That boy!

Amigo sits,
Quiet as a stone,
And sees the boy
Walking alone
And carrying a heavy pail
Of water down the rocky trail
And singing.
Ah, what a sound!
Amigo found
It going round
His head all day.
It would not go away—
That sound of singing,
Ringing
In his head.

He said,
"I know every sound for miles around,
Every small and quiet sound—
Like earthworms walking underground
And the whisper of quail
And the wet creaking wail
Of baby toads after a rain,
And the rustle of grass
Where a deer has lain
Yes,
I think there's many a sound
Pleasant enough to have around."

"But
Human boys
Make the finest
Kind of noise
I ever heard—
Better than water
Or wind or bird."

This boy was a little thing—
Only so high.
But he seemed to Amigo
To reach the sky,
Tall as a mountain,
Brown and strong.
Amigo followed him
All day long.

323

He heard his whistle
And he heard his song
Carried by the wind,
Light as a feather.

Amigo said,
"I wonder whether
He ever saw me
Peeping from under

That mesquite tree
And popping up
From clumps of grass
Along the way
To see him pass."

But his mother said,
"Be careful, my child.
A human boy
Is very wild."

Amigo said,
"I'll tame him if it takes a year.
The sound of that boy is all I want to hear!"

"You can't mean that!
Better go play with the
Old pack rat."

The prairie dogs listened
With great surprise.
You could tell what they thought
By the look in their eyes.
One finally said, as he gazed at the sun,
"Better learn from those who are wise, little one.
Mountain is your friend.
Wind is your toy.
Let's stop this talk about
A human boy."

A hundred aunts, uncles and cousins agreed.
"That's right," they said,
And they wiggled their whiskers
And nodded their heads.
"Oh, yes, that's right," they said.
"That's right."

But Amigo told them,
"He doesn't look wild
I know if I try
I can tame that child."

"How about an ant?"

"An ant?
I can't
Love an ant.
I just can't."

"How about a bee
With a lazy buzz?"

"No. I don't like honey
And he does."

"Play with a cricket.
Play with a quail
Tame you a lizard
With a sandy tail."

"They're all good friends
But they're just not boys
And they can't make
That fine boy-noise."

Amigo tried to make them understand.
"I'm as much a part of the desert land
As any mountain or grain of sand,
Or soft quail cry
Or sunset sky
Or dust-devil blowing high
As a bird.
And that boy
Is a part of it too—
The same as I.
He's a desert thing like any other.
Sometimes I think he is my brother."

Amigo's mother nodded her head.
"Taming a boy seems odd," she said.
"It's never been done, as far as I know,
But no one ever loved one so—
And that makes all the difference.
You may be the one
Who will do it, my son."

"The thing to do now
Is tame him.
But how?
What can I give him?
I wish I knew.
I have no treasures,
Not even a few."

"Just give him something
That pleases you."

"Like silvery sand
To hold in his hand?
Or the blue jay feather
That floated down
Straight from the sky
To Prairie-Dog Town?
Or that cool green shadowy grass
Which grows so tall at the mountain pass
And tastes of mountain water?"

His mother said, "These
Would surely please
A boy."

So Amigo scampered
And ran and hopped.
The sun was high
Before he stopped—
At the very top
Of the mountain pass,
Where all the grass
Was sweet as honey
And tall enough to hide in.
Amigo took great pride in
His work that day.

He sniffed a thousand blades of grass
Before he found the one
That smelled the most like mountain water—
And shone like mountain sun.

He took the green blade
Tenderly down
Into the valley near
Prairie-Dog Town.
And beside the path
Where the boy often came,
He placed the grass on a small white stone—
Which he always thought of
As his own.

As he waited he made a kind of game
Of dreaming the boy was already tame
And knew his name—
And said,
"Amigo."

But it was no game,
For the boy came along
Trailing his song
In the windy air.
And it was no dream,
For he saw Amigo there.
He did not speak.
He only sat
Very quietly gazing at
The world of sun and sand.
And when he left, a blade of grass
Was clutched in his brown hand.

And Amigo ran home
Bounding with joy,
Shouting, "Listen,
I've just about
Tamed me a boy!"

At the same time,
On the same day,
You could hear
Francisco say,
"Mama, I know that he's
Just about mine!
Isn't that wonderful?
Isn't that fine?"

Francisco went back to the stone
Every day.
He was a friend
In every way.
He brought wild cherries
Gathered in the mountains
And fat dark berries
That grew on sandy banks.
To see Amigo eat them
Was all the thanks
He needed.
When the summer sun beat fiercely down
And the heat lay heavy on Prairie-Dog Town,
He found a rock shaped like a cup
And every morning he filled it up
With water.

And he kept one eye on the sky
To warn Amigo when hawks flew by.
And every day
Amigo came closer
To the place
Where Francisco sat—
As near as that.

The boy was taming Amigo.
Oh, yes,
That's so.
And if you were watching Amigo
You'd know
That he was taming Francisco.
And you would think
The boy wished he were tame
The way he came
Closer
And
Closer.

Francisco took the presents
Amigo left here and there.
He even stuck that blue jay
Feather in his hair.

Many a time
The boy would lie down
In the tall wispy grass
Near Prairie-Dog Town,
Quiet as field mouse in its nest,
Like any desert creature taking a rest.
Amigo liked knowing that he was near.
He listened for his whistle in the summer air—
And sure enough the whistle was there!

Amigo ran
Close to the sound.
Francisco smiled,
Turned around
And met Amigo.

That was the way
It happened that day.
First they climbed a hill.
They followed a bee.
Then they stopped to rest
By a mesquite tree.
They didn't talk much for the wind was shrill.
They sat there quietly, as good friends will,
Admiring the view from the rocky hill.

Now
Francisco thought,
"I've tamed me a prairie dog.
He's my greatest joy."
And
Amigo thought
"Mine is the *best* pet.
I've tamed me a boy."

Amigo squeaked a happy sound,
And when he was through
Francisco said, "Yes,
I think so too."

Key to Pronunciation

Letter Symbol for a sound	Key Word and Its Respelling	Letter Symbol for a sound	Key Word and Its Respelling
a	pat (PAT)	ch	church (CHERCH)
ah	far (FAHR)	hw	when (HWEN)
ai	air (AIR)	ks	mix (MIKS)
aw	jaw (JAW)	kw	quick (KWIK)
ay	pay (PAY)	ng	thing (THING)
e	pet (PET)		finger (FING-gər)
ee	bee (BEE)	sh	shoe (SHOO)
ehr	berry (BEHR-ee)	ss	case (KAYSS)
er	term (TERM)	th	thing (THING)
i	pit (PIT)	th̲	this (TH̲IS)
igh	sigh (SIGH)	zh	pleasure (PLEZH-ər)
ihr	pier (PIHR)		
o	pot (POT)		
oh	oh, boat (BOHT)		
oi	oil (OIL)		
oo	boot, rule (ROOL)		
or	for (FOR)		
ow	power (POW-ər)		
u	put, book (BUK)		
uh	cut (KUHT)		
y	used in place of (igh) before two consonant letters as in child (CHYLD)		
ə	represents the sound for any vowel spelling when a syllable is sounded very weakly, as in the first syllable of about, or the last syllables of item, gallop, or focus, or the middle syllable of charity		

Glossary

ac·cuse (ə-KYOOZ) 1. To say someone has done wrong: Are you going to *accuse* Ted of taking your book ? **accused, accusing.**

ad An advertisement. A public notice telling about the good qualities of something for sale: If you look in the newspaper, you may find an *ad* for the kind of dog you want.

ad·mit (ad-MIT) 1. To let someone enter: I cannot *admit* you without a ticket. 2. To confess: Joe *admits* that he is afraid to go into the old house. **admitted, admitting.**

af·fect (ə-FEKT) 1. To bring about a change in: Rainfall *affects* the growth of plants. 2. To arouse emotion: Sad movies *affect* me. **affected, affecting.**

al·li·ga·tor (AL-ə-gay-ter) 1. A large reptile with a broad nose, long tail, scaly hide, and sharp teeth: *Alligators* live in swamps and rivers of southeastern United States.

al·lo·sau·rus (al-ə-SAWR-uhss) A dinosaur; a meat-eating reptile of long ago.

ant·ler (ANT-lər) One of two large branched horns on the head of an animal of the deer family.

ar·mor (AHR-mər) 1. Any safe covering: The turtle carries a shell of *armor.* 2. A metal covering, like a suit, worn for protection in battle. **armored, armoring.**

a·ston·ish (ə-STON-ish) To fill with wonder: It would *astonish* me if we won first prize. **astonished, astonishing.**

bad·ger (BAJ-ər) 1. A short-legged, furry animal that lives in a hole in the ground. 2. To pester or bother: Don't *badger* me while I work. **badgered, badgering.**

bait (BAYT) 1. Food placed on a hook or trap to catch fish and other animals. 2. Something used to trick a person: The money was left on the table as *bait* to catch the thief. 3. To place food on a hook or in a trap: Please *bait* my hook with a worm. 4. To tease: I saw the boy *bait* the old dog by holding a bone. **baited, baiting.**

ban·quet (BANG-kwit) A feast in honor of a person, group, or special day.

bare·back (BAIR-bak) On a horse's bare back without a saddle: Riding *bareback* is not easy.

bass (BASS) A kind of fish found in either fresh or salt water. **bass or basses.**

bay 1. An inlet of a body of water. 2. A deep bark: The hunter heard the *bay* of his dog. 3. A reddish-brown color. 4. To bark: Have you ever heard a wolf *bay* at the moon? **bayed, baying.**

beam (BEEM) 1. A large, strong piece of wood or metal used to hold up a building. 2. A stream of light. 3. The greatest width of a ship. 4. To smile: My little sister *beams* whenever I give her a new toy. **beamed, beaming.**

bel·low (BEL-oh) 1. To make a loud, deep sound or outcry: He began to *bellow* orders to the crew. 2. A loud, deep shout: The giant cried out in a deep *bellow.* **bellowed, bellowing.**

bleat (BLEET) 1. The noise or cry made by sheep or goats, or a sound like it: the *bleat* of a goat. 2. To make the noise or cry made by sheep or goats: The goat *bleats* loudly. **bleated, bleating.**

bliz·zard (BLIZ-ərd) A heavy snowstorm with strong, cold winds.

blur (BLER) 1. To smear: Rain will *blur* your ink drawing. 2. To make unclear in outline: If you move the camera, the picture will *blur.* 3. To darken or dim: We watched the fog *blur* the lighthouse beam. 4. A smear or blot: The car was going so fast that all we saw was a *blur.* **blurred, blurring.**

bon·bon (BON-bon) A piece of candy, usually soft with a fancy shape.

bore (BOR) 1. A person or thing that is dull or not interesting: The movie was a *bore.* 2. To make a hole by drilling: *Bore* a hole in the wood for the screw. 3. To become tired with things that are not interesting: People who talk about the same thing all the time *bore* me. **bored, boring.**

bron·to·saur·us (brahn-tə-SAWR-uhss) A huge dinosaur that lived long ago in North America.

broth 1. A soup made from water in which meat, chicken, and/or vegetables have been boiled. 2. The water in which meat or vegetables have been boiled.

buck (BUHK) 1. A male animal, especially a deer. 2. To rear suddenly: The horse will *buck* until the rider falls off. 3. To oppose; go against. **bucked, bucking.**

buck·eye (BUHK-igh) 1. A tree belonging to the horse chestnut family with showy bunches of small flowers, large leaves, and large brown seeds. 2. The large brown seeds from the tree.

buz·zard (BUHZ-ərd) A type of bird that hunts other animals.

calf (KAF) 1. A young cow or bull. 2. The soft leather that comes from a young cow or bull. 3. The back part of the leg between the knee and the ankle. **calves** (KAVZ).

charm·ing (CHAHR-ming) Having charm; pleasing: Both of them are *charming* people.

chat 1. A relaxed talk: I had a nice *chat* with Mrs. Smith yesterday. 2. To talk in a relaxed way: Jane wants to *chat* with you before class. **chatted, chatting.**

cli·mate (KLIGH-mit) 1. The usual weather conditions of an area: Polar bears live in very cold *climates.* 2. An atmosphere or general feeling: a *climate* of joy. **climates.**

comb (KOHM) 1. A short thin piece of metal or plastic with a row of teeth used to fix or clean the hair. 2. A crest on the head of a rooster or other bird. 3. To untangle or fix with a comb. 4. To search or look for thoroughly: Dave *combed* the library looking for the right book. **combed, combing.**

con·crete (KON-kreet) 1. A mixture of cement with water and sand or gravel used for building: That tall building is made of *concrete.* 2. (kon-KREET) Solid, real.

con·duc·tor (kən-DUHK-tər) 1. A person who collects money or sells tickets on trains, buses, and so on. 2. A person who leads a band. 3. Something that carries or sends electricity, sound, or heat: Metal is a good *conductor* of heat.

con·tin·ue (kən-TIN-yoo) 1. To go on; keep doing: Please *continue* reading for as long as you want to. **continued, continuing.**

cor·ner (KOR-nər) 1. The spot where two streets or sidewalks meet: The group will meet at the *corner* of Main and First Streets at ten o'clock. 2. The place where two surfaces or lines come together: Chairs were placed in each *corner* of the room. 3. A faraway place: Many people have explored all *corners* of the Earth. 4. To force into a place from which there is no getting away: If the police can *corner* the robber, they can catch him. **cornered, cornering.**

cot (KOT) A lightweight, narrow bed.

coup·le (KUHP-əl) 1. Two together; a pair: Form a line in *couples.* 2. To join together: We watched the engine *couple* with the freight cars. 3. To pair off: *Couple* yourselves with someone who has the same number as you. **coupled, coupling.**

crab·by (KRAB-ee) Mean or cross.

cray·fish (KRAY-fish) Also **crawfish** 1. A fish that is like a lobster but smaller in size. 2. A small, spiny lobster.

creek (KREEK or KRIK) 1. A path of water smaller than a river; a stream. 2. An inlet or bay of small size.

croc·o·dile (KROK-ə-dighl) A large lizard-like reptile with a thick-skinned body, long powerful tail, and long-pointed noise. **crocodiles.**

de·tec·tive (di-TEK-tiv) One whose job it is to find secret facts or solve crimes, often working with or for the police. **detectives.**

dia·mond (DIGH-mənd or DIGH-ə-mənd) 1. A very hard stone of much worth. 2. A figure with four equal angled sides. 3. A playing card which has such a figure on it. 4. A baseball field.

dim 1. Not bright: The light was so *dim* that we could hardly see each other. 2. Not clear: He has a *dim* memory of his childhood. 3. To make less bright: *Dim* the lights so we can see the movie. **dimmer, dimmest, dimmed, dimming, dimly.**

di·no·saur (DIGH-nə-sor) One of the class of long-tailed reptiles that lived millions of years ago.

dis·tant (DISS-tənt) 1. Far away in time or space, as a distant country. 2. Cool or not friendly: It's hard to make friends with a *distant* person.

e·rupt (ih-RUHPT) To break out or burst forth as lava and hot ash do from a volcano. **erupted, erupting.**

ev·er·green (EV-ər-green) A tree, shrub, or other plant that stays green all through the year.

fate (FAYT) 1. What some people believe causes things to happen: John believed *fate* would bring him much money, but Bill believed in hard work. 2. An outcome that cannot be helped: It was Joan's *fate* to be chosen the leader.

fid·dle (FID-l) 1. A violin. 2. To play a violin. 3. To act in a restless way: We can't hear the movie if you *fiddle* with that piece of paper. **fiddled, fiddling.**

fin 1. A thin, winglike or bladelike part of the body of a fish or certain other animals. 2. Any part that is like the fin of a fish: The rocket's *fins* keep it moving straight.

flip·per (FLIP-ər) 1. A flat, broad fin used for swimming by animals such as seals and whales. 2. (Usually plural) Rubber devices for the feet in the shape of fins, used for swimming.

fos·sil (FOSS-l) The remains or imprint of a plant or animal.

frame (FRAYM) 1. The enclosing edge of a picture, door, or window. 2. The parts of a building that hold everything up or together: the *frame* of a house. 3. The (human) body; skeleton. 4. To make a frame. 5. To put a frame on or around: *frame* a picture. **framed, framing.**

gill (GIL) The part of the body that permits fish and other animals to breathe in water.

glance (GLANSS) 1. A fast look: Shirley was in a hurry and had only a *glance* at the parade. 2. To take a fast look: I saw him *glance* at me and then turn away. **glanced, glancing, glances.**

glide (GLIGHD) To move smoothly: Watch the sea gulls as they *glide* over the water. **glided, gliding.**

glum (GLUHM) 1. Not happy; sad: Pat is *glum* because the game was called off.

gnash (NASH) To grind (the teeth) together: Do you *gnash* your teeth at night ? **gnashed, gnashing.**

gob·ble (GOB-əl) 1. To eat very fast: You should not *gobble* your food so fast. 2. To make a noise like a turkey. **gobbled, gobbling.**

gog·gles (GOG-əlz) Eyeglasses worn to protect the eyes; safety glasses.

grav·el (GRAV-əl) Small pieces of stone: Many walks and roads are made with *gravel.*

greed·y (GREED-ee) 1. Wanting more than one has need for: *greedy* for money. 2. Having a great want for food.

han·dle (HAN-dl) 1. That part of an object to be held or turned. 2. To touch, move, or hold with the hands: *Handle* the kitten gently. 3. To manage or control. **handled, handling, handles.**

hull (HUHL) 1. The main part of the body of a ship. 2. The outer covering of a seed, fruit, or nut. 3. To remove the covering of a seed or fruit. **hulled, hulling.**

knap·sack (NAP-sak) A bag or pack made of heavy cloth for carrying things on the back: We can carry sleeping bags in our *knapsack.*

lab·o·ra·to·ry (LAB-ə-rə-tor-ee) A room or building used for scientific work. **laboratories.**

la·dle (LAYD-l) 1. A spoon with a long handle and large bowl, used for serving 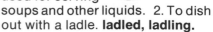 soups and other liquids. 2. To dish out with a ladle. **ladled, ladling.**

lamp·post (LAMP-pohst) A post that holds a street lamp.

las·so (LASS-oh) 1. A long rope with a slip knot that forms a loop at one end, used for catching cattle or horses. 2. To catch with a lasso. **lassos** or **lassoes, lassoed, lassoing.**

log·ger (LAW-gər) 1. Someone who cuts down trees. 2. A machine that loads logs.

lug (LUHG) To drag or pull with much trouble: Joe had to *lug* the heavy suitcase up the steps. **lugged, lugging.**

lum·ber (LUHM-bər) 1. Sawed logs ready for use; boards. 2. To move in a noisy or clumsy way: Bears sometimes *lumber* through the woods. **lumbered, lumbering.**

ma·ple (MAY-pəl) 1. A shade tree, one type of which produces the sap used in making maple syrup. 2. The wood of the maple tree. **maples.**

mer·maid (MER-mayd) In fairy tales, a creature with the head and upper body of a woman, but the lower body of a fish.

min·now (MIN-oh) A small freshwater fish.

mod·est (MOD-ist) 1. Shy; bashful. 2. Not showy in one's dress or behavior; She is *modest* about her work. **modestly.**

moon·beam (MOON-beem) A stream of moonlight.

mum·ble (MUHM-bəl) 1. To speak in a way that cannot be heard or understood, as with the mouth almost closed: The shy child *mumbles* often. **mumbled, mumbling, mumbles.**

mums (MUHMZ) Chrysanthemums. A large flower or the plant on which it grows: Some *mums* are yellow and some are white.

mus·tang (MUHSS-tang) A wild horse of the plains of North America.

nail (NAYL) 1. A hard, slender piece of painted metal used to hold together materials such as wood. 2. A fingernail or toenail. 3. To hold together with a nail or nails: We can *nail* the picture on the wall. **nailed, nailing.**

nei·ther (NEE-thər or NIGH-thər) 1. Not either: *Neither* shoe is wet. 2. Not either one: *Neither* of us likes baseball. 3. Nor: Dad doesn't smoke; *neither* does Mother.

nib·ble (NIB-əl) 1. To eat or chew with quick, small bites. 2. To eat small bits slowly: We always *nibble* popcorn at the movies. 3. A small bite; quick small bites. **nibbled, nibbling, nibbles.**

oar·lock (OR-lock) An object, often u-shaped, on the side of a boat to hold the oar in place. **oarlocks.**

or·di·nary (ORD-n-ehr-ee) 1. Usual: My *ordinary* bedtime is nine o'clock. 2. Common, not special.

os·trich (OSS-trich or AWSS-trich) 1. A large, long-legged bird that cannot fly, often found in Asia and Africa where it is dry: An *ostrich* can run fast because of its powerful legs.

pad·dle (PAD-l) 1. A short pole with a broad blade, used with both hands to move a boat through the water. 2. Anything shaped like this, often used for striking or beating: Ping-Pong *paddle.* 3. To move through water with a paddle or with a paddle-like motion. 4. To move about (in the water) by moving the hands and feet quickly. **paddled, paddling, paddles.**

pa·le·on·tol·o·gist (pay-lee-on-TOL-ə-jist) A person who studies fossils and very old forms of life.

pars·ley (PAHRSS-lee) A plant with small bright green curly leaves, often used to flavor food.

pep·per (PEP-ər) 1. The small berry of a vine used ground or whole as a sharp flavoring in food. 2. A bell-shaped food tasting anywhere from mild to hot and differing in color from red to green. 3. To sprinkle with pepper. 4. To hit rapidly with small objects. **peppered, peppering.**

pet·ri·fy (PET-rə-figh) 1. To turn into stone. 2. To stun with fear or some other strong feelings: Bill *petrifies* his friends with ghost stories. **petrified, petrifying.**

pier (PIHR) A structure built on posts out over water and used as a dock or a walk.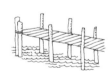

plas·ter (PLASS-tər) 1. A thick, sticky mixture which is spread on walls and ceilings where it dries to a hard surface. 2. To cover with plaster; to spread (anything) as if using plaster. 3. To cover fully or widely: Let's *plaster* the wall with pictures. **plastered, plastering.**

plunge (PLUNJ) 1. To dive or rush into: *Plunge* into the pool. 2. To push something quickly into: The cook *plunges* the lobster into hot water. 3. To rush forward or downward: We watched the car *plunge* down the steep hill. 4. A dive or sudden push forward or downward: We went for a *plunge* in the pool. **plunged, plunging.**

pod A shell that holds the seeds of a plant: *peapod.*

pol·ish (POL-ish) 1. To make or become smooth and shiny: *Polish* the floor. 2. To make better or finish: *Polish* a report. 3. That which is used to make something smooth and shiny: shoe *polish.* 4. Shininess: the *polish* of silver. **polished, polishing, polishes.**

quiv·er (KWIV-ər) 1. To shake or bring about a slight shaking; tremble: His lower lip began to *quiver* when he heard the sad news. 2. A slight shaking. 3. A case used to hold arrows. **quivered, quivering.**

rare (RAIR) 1. Not often found; unusual: a *rare* illness. 2. Very special: a *rare* skill. 3. Very thin, as air: The air was *rare* at the top of the mountain. 4. Not well-cooked: Do you like your beef *rare* ? **rarer, rarest, rarely.**

rear (RIHR) 1. The back part: the *rear* of a bus. 2. Of or at the back: the *rear* door. 3. To rise on hind legs: The horse started to *rear* in fright. **reared, rearing.**

rec·i·pe (RESS-ə-pee) A set of directions for preparing anything, especially food. **recipes.**

rep·tile (REP-til or REP-tighl) A cold-blooded animal that has a backbone and moves by creeping or crawling: Snakes, lizards, turtles, and alligators are *reptiles.*

re·spon·si·bil·i·ty (ri-spon-sə-BIL-ə-tee) 1. The state of being responsible: Chris accepted the *responsibility* of caring for his dog. 2. A person or thing for which someone is responsible.

re·spon·si·ble (ri-SPON-sə-bəl) 1. Having a duty toward something: Parents are *responsible* for raising their children. 2. Being the cause of: The broken machine was *responsible* for the loud noise. 3. Having many things that must be done: a *responsible job.* 4. Able to accept duties; worthy of trust: The most *responsible* worker will get the job. **responsibly.**

rip·ple (RIP-əl) 1. A very small wave: The rain caused *ripples* to appear on the pond. 2. To make very small waves: The breeze *ripples* the surface of the pond. **rippled, rippling, ripples.**

route (ROOT or ROWT) 1. The road or way to go. 2. A way that follows a usual pattern or is made up of actions at a series of places: newspaper *route.* 3. To send along the usual road or way: We will *route* you the shortest way. **routed, routing, routes.**

rus·set (RUHSS-ət) 1. Yellowish-brown; reddish-brown. 2. A rough russet-colored cloth. 3. A kind of apple with a brownish skin.

scale (SKAYL) 1. One of the many hard, flat plates that cover certain animals, especially reptiles and fish. 2. An object used for weighing. 3. Eight notes in music that follow one another. 4. To climb: *Scale* a ladder. 5. To remove scales from: You can *scale* a fish before you cook it. **scaled, scaling, scales.**

scoop (SKOOP) 1. A spoon-like kitchen tool for lifting sugar, flour, or ice cream. 2. That which fills a scoop: He took out three *scoops* of ice cream. 3. To lift out or up, as with a scoop: *Scoop* the ball off the ground. **scooped, scooping.**

scut·tle (SKUHT-l) To run with quick movements; to scamper. **scuttled, scuttling.**

sep·a·rate (SEP-ə-rayt) 1. To keep apart by putting something between: Draw a line to *separate* your side from mine. 2. To put into different groups: We can *separate* the red jellybeans from the green ones. 3. To part: We are never going to find him if we do not *separate.* 4. (SEP-ə-rit) Not joined; not shared; apart: The garage is *separate* from the house. **separated, separating, separately.**

shab·by (SHAB-ee) 1. Worn-out: This coat is so *shabby* that I can't wear it anymore. 2. Wearing old, worn clothing: a *shabby* tramp. **shabbier, shabbiest, shabbily.**

shade (SHAYD) 1. The darkness brought about when an object cuts off the light from the sun or anything else: the *shade* of a tree. 2. An object used to block or cut off the light: a window *shade.* 3. How light or dark a color is: many *shades* of green. 4. To block from light: *Shade* yourself from the sun, or you might get a bad sunburn. **shaded, shading.**

shal·low (SHAL-oh) 1. Not deep: a *shallow* stream. 2. Not deep or careful (in thought): Because he does not think carefully, people say he is a *shallow* person.

shrub (SHRUHB) A woody plant that has many stems beginning at its base; a bush.

shrug (SHRUHG) 1. To raise the shoulders for a short moment, as if to show uncertainty or no interest. 2. The motion of raising the shoulders for a short moment: He gave a *shrug* when I asked him if he wanted to go to the game. **shrugged, shrugging.**

shud·der (SHUHD-ər) 1. To shake suddenly: I began to *shudder* when I heard a noise outside. 2. A sudden shaking. **shuddered, shuddering.**

shut·ter (SHUHT-ər) 1. A door-like covering hung on each side of a window or doorway. 2. A flap in front of a camera lens.

sim·mer (SIM-ər) 1. To boil gently. 2. To cook just at the boiling point.

sire (SIGHR) 1. A father or grandfather. 2. A four-legged animal's father. **sires.**

skel·e·ton (SKEL-ə-tən) 1. The bones as the framework of a body. 2. A framework or outline of something. **skeletal.**

slith·er (SLITH-ər) To move in a sliding, slipping, or gliding motion: Did you see the snake *slither* in the grass? **slithered, slithering.**

sly (SLIGH) 1. Smart; able to fool others. 2. Secret; sneaky: The

robber was very *sly*. **slier** or **slyer, sliest** or **slyest, slyly, slyness.**

snif·fle (SNIF-l) To sniff over and over, as when one is crying or has a cold. **sniffled, sniffling.**

snooze (SNOOZ) 1. To take a nap; to sleep. 2. A nap. **snoozed, snoozing.**

snort 1. To force air through the nose with a sudden loud sound to show surprise, dislike, or anger: Can you *snort* like a bull? 2. The act or sound of snorting: The bull gave an angry *snort* and then charged. **snorted, snorting.**

soothe (SOOTH) 1. To calm: Soft music *soothes* me. 2. To lessen pain or worry: A cool cream will *soothe* my sunburn. **soothed, soothing.**

speck·le (SPEK-əl) 1. A dot or small spot; a speck. 2. To dot with specks: My dress is *speckled* with green dots. **speckled, speckling.**

spell (SPEL) 1. To say or write out the letters that make up a word. 2. A state of being in the power of magic: Because she was under a *spell,* Sleeping Beauty slept for many years. 3. A time: a hot *spell.*

spike (SPIGHK) 1. A large, thick nail. 2. Any sharp, pointed object that sticks out: Tulip *spikes* push up through  the earth. 3. To join with a spike or put a spike into. **spiked, spiking.**

sput·ter (SPUHT-ər) 1. To make hissing, spitting noises. 2. To talk in a way that is difficult to understand. **sputtered, sputtering.**

squash (SKWOSH) 1. A fruit that grows on a vine and is used as a vegetable. 2. To crush or mash: Did you *squash* the strawberry on the floor? 3. The act or sound of squashing: I heard a *squash* when I stepped on the tomato. 4. A game played by hitting a ball against walls with rackets. **squashed, squashing.**

squirm (SKWERM) To twist the body this way and that: I felt the worm *squirm* in my hand. **squirmed, squirming.**

squirt (SKWERT) 1. To shoot out suddenly in a jet: This toy gun *squirts* water. **squirted, squirting.**

star·tle (STAHRT-l) To bring about sudden fright or movement; to surprise: We were *startled* by the noise in the woods. **startled, startling.**

stomp 1. To step or stamp heavily with the bottom of the foot: Everyone started to *stomp* to the music. 2. A heavy step or stamping. **stomped, stomping.**

stove·pipe (STOHV-pighp) 1. A metal pipe to carry smoke or fumes from a stove into the chimney. 2. A tall hat made of silk.

stud·y (STUHD-ee) 1. To try to learn: You must *study* for the test tomorrow. 2. To look at carefully: Babies *study* colorful objects. 3. A subject or field: Astronomy is the *study* of the stars, planets, and outer space. 4. A room used for reading or studying. **studied, studying, studies.**

swamp (SWAHMP or SWAWMP) 1. Soft, wet land. 2. To sink; flood; fill with water: The big wave is going to *swamp* the boat. **swamped, swamping, swampy.**

swell (SWEL) 1. To become bigger and bigger: A broken finger often *swells.* 2. To become filled (with pride): Did your head *swell* when you won the race? 3. A large wave or group of waves. **swelled** or **swollen, swelling.**

swing 1. To move back and forth in a free swaying motion: The tree branches *swing* in the breeze. 2. A swinging movement, used to hit an object: She took a *swing* at the punching bag. 3. A seat, hung from above by chains or ropes, on which one moves back and forth through the air. **swung, swinging.**

switch (SWICH) 1. A stick used for whipping or beating. 2. Something to turn electricity on or off. 3. A change or shift. 4. To move back and forth like a switch: A horse *switches* his tail to chase the flies away. **switched, switching.**

swoop (used with *down*) 1. To move quickly through the air: The owl *swooped* down on the mouse. 2. The act of swooping; a sudden, quick attack. **swooped, swooping.**

tack·le (TAK-əl) 1. (Football) To jump on or seize in order to stop. 2. The act of tackling. 3. Something needed for special sports, especially fishing. 4. A position on a football team. **tackled, tackling, tackles.**

351

theme (THEEM) 1. The main idea in a story, play, or other work. 2. A short written story. 3. The main melody in a musical work.

thrash 1. To beat; give a whipping to. 2. To move (arms and legs) about in a forceful way: They saw the fish *thrash* in the water. **thrashed, thrashing.**

thrill (THRIL) 1. A feeling of great excitement: Winning the race was a *thrill.* 2. To feel or cause to feel excitement: Does it *thrill* you to see a famous person? **thrilled, thrilling.**

tick (TIK) 1. A sound made by a clock or a watch: The *tick* of the clock kept me awake. 2. To make the sound of a tick or ticks, as a clock does: We heard the insect *ticking* in the grass. **ticked, ticking.**

tin·gle (TING-gəl) 1. To feel a slight stinging, as from the cold, or a slap, or excitement: My fingers *tingle* from the cold. 2. A slight sting: The scary movie gave me a *tingle.* **tingled, tingling.**

tow·head (TOH-hed) A person with very light pale-yellow hair.

trach·o·don (TRAK-ə-don) A dinosaur with a long wide tail that lived in or near the water and ate only plants and leaves.

tri·cer·a·tops (trigh-SEHR-ə-tops) A dinosaur that ate only plants and leaves and had three horns on its head.

troop 1. A group of persons, animals, or things. 2. (Usually plural): A group of soldiers. 3. To go or walk, usually in a group: The students *troop* out of the classroom. **trooped, trooping.**

trout (TROWT) Any of a type of freshwater fish. **trout.**

ty·ran·no·sau·rus (ti-ran-ə-SAWR-uhss) A large flesh-eating dinosaur that walked on its hind legs.

vet Veterinarian. A doctor who cares for animals.

wade (WAYD) 1. To walk through water or something that slows movement: They had to *wade* through mud to get to the other side. **waded, wading.**

whisk (HWISK) 1. (Used with *away, off,* or *out*) To grab, brush, or move quickly with a sweeping movement: When the magician *whisks* away the scarf, a chicken will appear! 2. A wire object used in cooking for beating a liquid. **whisked, whisking.**

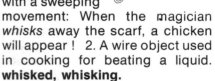

wit 1. (Often plural) Ability to learn or understand: Jack used his *wits* when his little brother was bitten by a dog. 2. A sense of humor: Janice has a sharp *wit.* 3. A person with a good sense of humor.

wob·ble (WOB-əl) 1. To move from side to side in an unsteady way: Babies *wobble* when they start to walk. 2. An unsmooth movement. **wobbled, wobbling.**